P9-BJC-066

On War and Writing

WITHDRAWN

ALSO BY SAMUEL HYNES

The Unsubstantial Air: American Fliers in the First World War

The Growing Seasons: An American Boyhood before the War

The Soldiers' Tale: Bearing Witness to Modern War

A War Imagined: The First World War and English Culture

Flights of Passage: Recollections of a World War II Aviator

The Auden Generation: Literature and Politics in England in the 1930s

Edwardian Occasions: Essays on English Writing
in the Early Twentieth Century

The Edwardian Turn of Mind

The Pattern of Hardy's Poetry

On War and Writing

SAMUEL HYNES

The University of Chicago Press
Chicago and London

The University of Chicago Press, Chicago 60637
The University of Chicago Press, Ltd., London
© 2018 by Samuel Hynes
All rights reserved. No part of this book may be used
or reproduced in any manner whatsoever without
written permission, except in the case of brief
quotations in critical articles and reviews. For more
information, contact the University of Chicago Press,
1427 East 60th Street, Chicago, IL 60637.

Published 2018
Printed in the United States of America

27 26 25 24 23 22 21 20 19 18   1 2 3 4 5

ISBN-13: 978-0-226-46878-5 (cloth)
ISBN-13: 978-0-226-46881-5 (e-book)
DOI: 10.7208/chicago/9780226468815.001.0001

Library of Congress Cataloging-in-Publication Data

Names: Hynes, Samuel, 1924– author.
Title: On war and writing : essays and introductions / Samuel Hynes.
Description: Chicago ; London : The University of Chicago Press, 2018. |
Includes bibliographical references and index.
Identifiers: LCCN 2017035132 | ISBN 9780226468785 (cloth : alk. paper) |
ISBN 9780226468815 (e-book)
Subjects: LCSH: War and literature. | War in literature. | World War,
1914–1918—Literature and the war. | World War, 1939–1945—Literature
and the war. | Literature, Modern—20th century—History and criticism. |
English literature—20th century—History and criticism.
Classification: LCC PN56.W3 H96 2018 | DDC 809/.933581—dc23
LC record available at https://lccn.loc.gov/2017035132

♾ This paper meets the requirements of ANSI/NISO
Z39.48-1992 (Permanence of Paper).

To Alan Thomas

Contents

Preface

This book is a gathering of pieces written over many years, in various forms, and on many different occasions—as essays, as introductions, as talks, as reviews—but with one common subject, War in the Twentieth Century, and more specifically the two World Wars. Those great wars changed the world, and the lives of the men who fought in them, and of those who lived in the aftermath. We in the twenty-first century live differently, and think differently, because those wars were fought.

A reader of these pieces will find many voices testifying to their wars—both young men who fought and civilians who only imagined. And one other voice, my own. I fought as a very young Marine in my generation's war, and I found, in the long teaching career that followed, that war remained in my mind, an ever-interesting subject that I returned to again and again. I have not attempted to update the pieces I wrote; they stand, each in its own moment, reflecting that moment's ideas about wars past, present, and to come.

To each piece, I have attached a note giving the date and place of its first publication. Three of the essays first appeared in the *Sewanee Review*, and I thank then-editor George Core for his friendship and support. I also thank the editors of the *New York Times Book Review*, the University of Toronto Press, the

(London) *Times Literary Supplement, Poetry*, Penguin Books, *MHQ: The Quarterly Journal of Military History*, and Presses de l'UFR Clerc Université Picardie for publishing these pieces first in their pages. The introduction and "A Critic Looks at War" appear in print here for the first time.

Introduction

All my working life I've had two vocations—flying and pro-fessing. Sometimes one has dominated, sometimes the other; but they've always been there. The flying came first. Imagine a grammar school playground in Minneapolis, around 1934. It's recess, and kids are playing the usual playground games, girls playing hopscotch and boys tearing about playing pum-pum-pullaway. Over on the far side, four or five boys are swirl-ing around each other, darting in and out. They carry their arms stretched out wide, and as they run they make stutter-ing noises—ack-ack-ack—their imitation of machine-gun fire. They shout to each other: "I'm Eddie Rickenbacker!" "I'm the Red Baron!" If it's winter, they don't wear wooly knitted hats; instead, they wear leather flying helmets with goggles.

The game they're playing is Dogfight. Their heads are full of World War I flying images that they've gathered from mov-ies like *Wings* and *Dawn Patrol*, and from stories they've read about the Lafayette Escadrille, and from pulp magazines like *G-8 and His Battle Aces*. Those bits and pieces are all about Aces and Heroes; they don't add up to a true account of that war-in-the-air, but they're enough to stir those small boys. I'm one of them. We're caught up in the romance of flying and planes. When a sky-writing plane appears above us we stop and stare while it scrawls Coca-Cola on the sky. On Saturday mornings, we ride our bikes out to the city airport and lie in the grass on a knoll just outside the perimeter fence and watch the planes as they pass above us on their landing approaches. Not the commercial ones. The Navy has a reserve squadron on the field, and we've come to see and hear the Navy planes land, sleek and serious, so close we can see the oil streaks on their fuselages and the wheels coming down. It doesn't occur to me that I'll ever be inside one of those magnificent machines; it's enough just to see them, up close and in the air.

But in time I do fly. The war—my war—came, and I left my freshman year at the University of Minnesota and enlisted in the Naval Aviation program, where I learned to fly. I was commissioned in the Marine Corps as a Second Lieutenant (my first vocation), got married, and flew in the Pacific Theater. When the war ended, I returned to the university and took up my other vocation; I became a college teacher, taught academic subjects, and wrote academic books (though the pilot in me got restless if they were *too* academic).

While I was still an undergraduate, I joined a reserve squadron and on weekends flew fighter planes out over the farms and lakes of Minnesota. I then went to graduate school for a couple of years and got a teaching job at Swarthmore College, until the Korean War came and the Marine Corps recalled me to my first vocation. I was ordered to Marine Air Station Cherry Point in North Carolina and put to teaching new ROTC lieutenants to be air controllers. In my spare time, I borrowed planes from the Headquarters Squadron's line, where there were always a few clapped-out fighters parked. After a day's work, I went back to my wife and children in Married Officers' Quarters and wrote my dissertation on Thomas Hardy's poetry.

After the Korean War ended, I returned to Swarthmore and the Professor took over again. For a couple of decades, I did all the appropriate things: taught academic subjects, wrote academic books, and went to academic meetings where I read academic papers. But the Old Pilot hung around. Occasionally, the need to fly would grab me, and I'd drive out to a small airfield nearby and rent a Cessna and just fly around. And I began another first-vocation project: I started writing in a notebook things I remembered from my WWII days—anecdotes, dialogues, Marine things. I looked at that notebook the other day. There's a whole page of Marine obscenities, the lyrics to several dirty songs, and an account of being in an electrical thunderstorm at night over the China Sea. It's not a narrative, just a way of preserving details of what it was like in my flying war, while those memories were still alive.

For the next couple of decades, that was my life: I taught, and I wrote in the notebook (and occasionally I hired a light plane and practiced landings or did stalls—just to keep my hand in). And I began putting the notes in the book together, not into a history of the war, but rather a personal account that would make *my* war as real as I could make it. By the 1970s, I had a draft and sent it to my agent. He passed it around and sent me the rejection slips. I remember especially the one from William Maxwell, an editor at the *New Yorker*. He liked the book, he said, but he couldn't possibly publish a piece of a pro-war book at a time like this (it was 1973, the end of US troops in Vietnam). So I put the manuscript in a drawer and went back to my other vocation. Fifteen years later, the national mood had changed; I pulled the manuscript out, rewrote it, and this time found a publisher. It appeared as *Flights of Passage* in 1988.

A year or two later I retired, and my wife, Liz, and I visited our elder daughter, who had grown up in those decades and married an Englishman who was a former Royal Air Force pilot. They lived near an airfield on the south coast of England. My son-in-law and I decided to take a long-distance cross-country flight together, from Shoreham in Sussex across the English Channel, then east across northern France to Verdun and back. Our route would take us along what had been the Western Front in WWI.

It was a memorable flight: from Shoreham to Dover, and across the Channel where Louis Blériot had crossed, to Calais and Ypres and Passchendaele and the Messine Ridge, and Loos and Arras and the Vimy Ridge, and the Argonne Forest and Mametz Wood to Verdun, then back by way of Albert and the Somme to Amiens, and home. The landscape of war was still there, and above it all the unsubstantial air those first pilots had flown in. I recognized it all. When we got back, the Professor took over and wrote an article about the flight. But the Old Pilot stepped in, and from then on they worked together—the Pilot writing and the Professor looking over his shoulder, watching for split infinitives.

I'd always been curious about the Western Front, and now I knew what it had been like to fly above it. It was time to turn to the American pilots of 1914–18 who had flown there and try to recover what it had been like for them up there, not working from history books but from their own words: their letters, diaries, journals, and memoirs. I was curious about them, a curiosity that you might call genealogical. I'd been a pilot in World War II; these pilots a generation earlier were my ancestors in flying. I felt a kinship with them. Much of what I felt in the air they must have felt.

But in one important way they were different; they had no war-flying ancestors. When they began to fly and fight, the Wright Brothers' first flight at Kitty Hawk was only a little more than ten years in the past, and Blériot's flight across the Channel was only five years after. War-in-the-Air as a form of combat didn't exist, hadn't even been imagined. It would all have to be invented, everything about it—the planes, the flight training, the strategy, the tactics, the pilots themselves. I'd have to dis-

cover how all that inventing was done, not from military histories, but from the men themselves, one testimony at a time.

I didn't start this complicated project at once. There was my
other vocation to be pacified first, academic commitments to
be met. That took another ten years. Finally, the millennium
turned, and I addressed my big question: What had it been
like, back in World War I, to be those first pilots? And all the
other questions involved: Who were they? Where did they come
from? Why did they choose the flying war?

Because they were my flying ancestors, I was most curious
about how they learned to fly, back then when nobody was sure.
In the Blériot method, for example, the beginner *never* flew
with an instructor. On his first day, he was simply shown how
the controls worked, and then stuck on the little wicker stool
that served as the pilot's seat and told to taxi across the field.
If he managed that without damaging the plane, he was told
to do it again, faster (*plus vite*!). If he succeeded, he was told
to take off! Just a few feet up at first and down to earth again.
If he made it, he did it again, but went higher—and he was flying! That solitary method as I read about it scared the hell out
of me, but Billy Mitchell, the Commander of the American Air
Force, swore it was the best.

I was curious about what further instruction they had, and
where they were trained, and by whom. How many hours did
they have when they first soloed? How many did they have when
they flew their first flight over the Western Front? ("Hours" is
a shorthand description of a pilot's skills; if you have logged,
say, a thousand hours of flight time, you must be pretty good, or
at least good *enough* (or lucky enough). What were they taught?
How to fly at night? In clouds? Could they navigate? Or did they
just follow roads and rivers like any amateur? These were a
working pilot's questions; the answers explain behavior in the
air, and consequences. Sometimes they tell you why men die.

I was curious about the planes they flew. Pilots always want to know what it would be like to fly this plane or that one; I suppose at the backs of their minds is the question: Could *I* fly it? All flying is a test. It isn't simply that planes are machines that function well or less well; planes have personalities. They're friendly or hostile, straightforward or devious, easy or difficult to control, predictable or capricious. The planes those first war-pilots flew were built before aircraft design had settled down, before engineers had agreed on how many wings a plane should have or on which end of the engine the propeller belonged. (Lanoe Hawker, the great English pilot, was shot down by the German Manfred von Richthofen, not because he was a less skillful flier, but because the Red Baron's triplane could turn inside Hawker's pusher-engined DH-2.)

A latter-day pilot looks back at those planes a little nervously; they seem to have been put together in too much of a hurry, and without enough tests. Questions arise about them, about their construction and equipment, and about their characteristics: air speeds, ceilings, how these planes spin, stall, land. What instruments did they carry? What were the controls like? (Some of the small, single-engine planes had steering wheels instead of sticks; some had no ailerons; some didn't have a horizontal stabilizer in the tail.) How close was the gas tank to the cockpit? (Wood and canvas planes were quick to burn.) What would happen in a high-speed dive? (In a Nieuport, the fabric of the upper wing might peel right off, like the foil on a Hershey bar.)

If you're interested in planes, you're interested in accidents. There were lots of them—there always are in military flying. You take wild young recruits who don't believe that they will ever die and put them in charge of powerful machines that they haven't yet learned to control. And so they pile up. More pilots died in accidents than in combat in the First War. That was true in my war, too; it's true in every modern war that I know about. So accidents are an important part of the story. They illuminate an episode, or the character of a plane or of a pilot. The way a pilot crashes can tell you a lot about that pilot. And the same is true of an airplane.

I was curious about how they felt about flying—how they felt when they took off for the first time and saw the green earth recede below them, and felt the vast empty air surround them. What did they feel when they first looked down at *war*, spread out below them like a burning map? What did they feel when they first shot at an enemy plane? (At those speeds and distances, you would see distinctly the enemy pilot you were attacking; you'd know when you hit him.) Did they feel exhilaration? And did that feeling make the rest of it—the strain and the fear and the loss of friends—seem worthwhile?

Another question, this time, a social one (such as a society hostess might ask): Who were they? Where did they come from? What defined and distinguished them from all the other troops? It turned out they were mostly college students (*college men*, as they said in those days). That was Congress's idea. The congressmen seemed to feel that a pilot had to be smart and independent, a man who could make his own decisions up there alone at 5,000 feet. Making college a requirement narrowed the number of candidates (3% of Americans 18–21 years old were in college in 1917). Some Ivy League-colleges already had flying clubs going when the US declared war: at Harvard, Yale, and Princeton (sometimes against the wishes of the university president, like A. Lawrence Lowell of Harvard, who argued that Harvard men had always chosen Cavalry or Artillery). It also determined the pilots' class; they would be *gentlemen*. Or most of them would be. There would be a few determined country boys who hadn't been to college who would find ways to get into aviation anyway—by joining the French Service Aéronautique, or the RAF or RCAF, and later transferring to the US Air Service. The "gentlemen" called these guys Roughnecks, and were surprised at how many they found when they joined the French or British squadrons at the Front.

Not only would American pilots be gentlemen, they would also be athletes. Air Service recruiters wrote to university presidents urging them to encourage their student athletes to enlist in aviation, and many of them did. One example was Hobey Baker, Princeton's most famous athlete. He had graduated in 1914 and was working on Wall Street and bored with it when the war began. He learned to fly at the flight school at Mineola, on Long Island, and led a flight of student-pilots to Princeton to fly over the Yale game in the fall of 1916. The *Princetonian* was dazzled by the display—the largest flight of aircraft ever seen together (there were eleven!).

Gentlemen, therefore officers: all pilots would be commissioned when they got their wings—some would be *First* Lieutenants at once, apparently on the grounds that pilots should automatically be senior to mere ground officers. And they'd have special uniforms: like the old cavalry, breeches and boots. And spurs! Young American pilots encouraged that special look; they'd go down to Paris and have new uniforms tailored with especially pink gabardine trousers. (That custom continued into *my* war, when Air Force pilots wore pink pants, and took the grommets out of their dress hats so they drooped over their ears.)

What this amounted to was a distinct pilot culture, consciously separated from the rest of the Army by class and background. They'd know each other; they'd have been together at Choate or Groton, or at Harvard or Yale; they'd speak the same language. It was something like being a fraternity man at a house party that never ended, or a college man on the Grand Tour.

Because many of them were athletes, they tended to see war-flying as a game, and talked and wrote about it that way: it's "a new game," "the best game over there," "a wicked old game"; or "it's a glorious sport," "the only sport there is." It's like the other games they've known in that it requires strenuous physical action, has rules and an opponent, requires special equipment and a (huge) space to play it in, and ends with a score (of planes shot down), somebody winning and somebody losing. Pilots who had trained and been commissioned had made the team (the poor guys on the ground hadn't), and sooner or later they would play their Big Game and win. The meaning of the metaphor will change as they learn the real rules of the game, and the cost of playing it, but to the end they'll call it "the flying game."

The Game was more than costume and equipment and rules: it spread over their lives, as style, a way of behaving. They took chances in the air, tried maneuvers they hadn't been taught—a loop or a hammerhead stall—just to see if they could do it, or tried a bit of low-level flat-hatting at treetop level, and boasted afterward that they'd "gotten away with it." "Getting away with it" applied to life on the ground, too, to parties in Paris and London, and women, and unauthorized nights in town. Here is John Grider, a planter's son from Arkansas, in London, writing to his hometown friend (and banker) Emma, explaining why he has just drawn $600 from an account that's empty:

I had a wonderful party at the Savoy last week and drew for six hundred. If you don't take care of me, I'll be put in jail. This London is *some* place, you would love it! I had dinner there several nights and all the women wear evening gowns, all the men in uniform, having fourteen days' leave from the front. It is some wild place.

Wild—in the minds of pilots like Grider, wildness is a virtue, not only at parties but everywhere in a pilot's life. They judge the desirability of one fighter squadron over another by how wild they are. Pilots in the US Air Service generally agreed that Rickenbacker's 94th was the best and wildest. Grider, who was with the RAF, thought Billy Bishop's 85 Squadron was the best, "a hard-fighting, hard-flying, hard-drinking lot of perfect princes."

They learned, in time, that wildness in the air was not the smart way to fight—learned it from more experienced pilots—like Rickenbacker and Raoul Lufbery—and from the hasty handbooks that some of those pilots wrote. In those books, they learned that the first law of aerial combat was *not* to be a hero but to survive—to figure the odds, and if they were against you, *scram*.

Lessons like that one changed the young pilots: those who didn't learn it didn't become old pilots. It was one of many changes, because war does change you, sends you home at the end not just an older person but a different one from the kid you were when you went—those of you who are veterans know that. Their values changed, their attitudes toward war changed. Even their vocabularies changed. They abandoned the Big Words of war—words like Hero and Chivalry, Bravery and Courage; leave them for the journalists, and the generals who write the medal citations. They settled for plain words—the names of pilots and of the planes they flew, and of the places where they died.

Their ideas of a life after the war changed, too. Once they had experienced flying war, they swore they could never go back to being what they'd been before, never join the family business or work at an office job. They'd known a life that was better than that, more exciting, active, personally theirs. Some joined one of the emerging commercial airlines, or became barnstormers, or opened flight schools. Others did go back, became their fathers, and never flew again, but maybe wrote a memoir, or a history of their squadron, and so kept that other vocation alive (as I did).

One last question: Why are war books important? I don't mean the military histories. I mean the personal accounts of the combatants, the ones I've been talking about. Because *war* is important, because it's always present in our world, dozens of wars being fought, somewhere, right now. Because war stirs young hearts. Because, as the great Eric Partridge wrote, war "next to love, has most captured the world's imagination."

We can never entirely imagine what it's like to actually fight a war—all war is unimaginable. The closest we can come is reading the personal records of men who were there, ordinary young guys, most of them, writing to their parents, or alone in their tents at night writing in a diary (which was forbidden), or old guys looking back, remembering what happened (like that thunderstorm over the China Sea), keeping alive a sense of what war is really like, when you're in it.

At War with Ken Burns

My hitch with Ken Burns's army began in August of 2002. That summer was a strange time in America. The papers I read at breakfast were full of war talk and ceremonial grief. In New York plans were being made for the first anniversary of the attack on the World Trade Center: there would be patriotic readings—the Gettysburg Address and the Declaration of Independence—and odes to the dead, and roses, and a marathon recitation of the names of all the victims. In Washington politicians were talking about a War on Terror, using the word *war* loosely and metaphorically—the way they used to talk about the War on Poverty and the War on Drugs—and President Bush was being briefed on how to stage a preemptive strike on Iraq. In Afghanistan American special forces were looking for Osama bin Laden. War was an oppressive presence, but it didn't seem real, more like a B-grade war movie. It would end after a while, the house lights would go up, and everybody would go home.

In the middle of all that unreality I was glad to get a letter from Lynn Novick, Ken Burns's coproducer. She and Ken were thinking about a PBS series about the American experience of the Second World War. Their planning had only begun, but they had two good working ideas to start with: they would build the film on the lives of ordinary people—the PFCs, not the generals—and they would include both the men who did the fighting and the folks who stayed home and worried. Would I like to join the company? It would be a relief, I thought, to escape from the fog of almost-war and go back in time to a real war. So I signed on.

More letters followed, explaining the project further, and setting a possible schedule. As they came, the intentions of the film seemed to expand; now it was to show "what the War meant then and means today and a great deal more." So there'd be two meanings, *then* and *now*, and more—though the letters didn't explain what that meant. The schedule would be leisurely; the first draft of the script wouldn't be finished until the fall of 2004. Editing would begin in 2007 or 2008. I liked that kind of planning: the film existed in an ideal state somewhere; but I wouldn't have to do any work for years.

The spacious plan didn't last long. By January 2003 the Burns staffers had found and interviewed some thirty people, scattered among four American towns, who remembered their war years; scriptwriting had begun, a first draft was expected in the fall of the year, and editing was now to begin in the spring of 2004. Nobody explained the acceleration, the sudden sense of urgency, if that's what it was.

The World War Two Film Project Board of Advisors (that's the title they gave us) met for the first time in New York in late February 2003. It was a very preliminary meeting, of all kinds of people—writers, editors, military historians, old veterans like me. And the Burns people—very bright and mostly very young, none of them old enough to have seen a serious war or to have lived through one, not even Vietnam. Together two or three generations of us shared what we remembered, or had discovered, and what we felt. By the end of the third day Ken and Lynn seemed confident that they knew enough to move on to the writing phase.

While we were meeting, the newspapers were full of a different war, the one that was in everyone's mind, but hadn't happened yet. The national mood, insofar as you would gauge it from the nineteenth floor of a building on Thirty-First Street, was edgy and uncertain; the air was full of lies and half-truths, of prevarications and mendacities and equivocations. The country seemed to have two options: to attack another country that was perhaps the wrong enemy, or to wait, anxiously and passively, for something worse to happen tomorrow or next week or maybe never.

But up on the nineteenth floor, the talk about *our* war was relaxed and easy. We knew how our story would run and how it would end. The good guys would win. And we knew for sure who the good guys were.

A few weeks later the war was in my morning *Times*:

BUSH ORDERS START OF WAR ON IRAQ;
MISSILES APPARENTLY MISS HUSSEIN

So the president had the war he wanted, and he had missed his first target.

The Ken Burns war went on. Researchers looked for more witnesses and more archival film and more statistics. Somebody sent me the transcript of the interview I'd done back in February, and I read it and sent it back, along with some old photographs of the young pilot I once was, back in our war. And the script grew.

In May another *Times* headline appeared: "BUSH DECLARES 'ONE VICTORY IN WAR ON TERROR.'" I saw the whole show on the evening news. There he came, striding across the flight deck of the aircraft carrier *Lincoln*; behind him a banner hung from the bridge announcing "Mission Accomplished." The president was dressed in a Navy flight suit; a leather patch sewn on his chest had Navy wings stamped on it and "*George W. Bush, Commander-in-Chief.*" That outfit made me sore. He had no right to be wearing Navy wings; he hadn't trained as a Navy pilot; he was Air Force, if he was anything. The whole performance made me uneasy; when was the last time an American president appeared dressed up in military clothes? And what comes next? A field marshal's uniform and a white horse? But it's all right: nobody takes him seriously, everybody laughs. There'll be no man on horseback in America, not any time soon.

In the fall (we're still in 2003) Lynn sends me the first draft of their fundraising proposal. The project has grown, both in length—it's now a five-part film, ten hours long—and in complexity of intention—now it's to be a "bottom up" exploration of the myriad ways in which World War II transformed our country, the war seen as a social force. The title has changed, too: it's no longer "The World War Two Film Project"; now it's simply "THE WAR." That's the way my generation has always thought of it; but what about younger people, who didn't grow up with it? Will they understand?

I respond to the draft a bit professorially. I object to the presence of high-velocity words like *agony* and *horror* and *gargantuan* and *fantastic* and *colossal*, and I am uncomfortable with sentences like this one: "Without sentimentality or nostalgia, the film will honor and celebrate the heroism, endurance, determination, sacrifice, and bravery of the generation of Americans who lived through it." Sentimentality and nostalgia—they'll be problems all right. Nostalgia, because when people my age look back at their war years they see their own youth, when they were free and full of life, excited by new places, new adventures, new skills, and new friends, when they were discovering for the first time how spacious the world is, how full of promises. And they forget, sometimes, what the war cost: not the money (there always seems to be plenty of money for war) but the destruction—the burning cities, the starving people, the sixty million dead, including a third of a million of their own generation who died violently and young.

And sentimentality, too, the kind that men feel (and maybe women, but mostly men) who come of age *after* a great war, knowing they were born too late ever to march to those brave drums. When you think of the scale of our war, and the absolute moral clarity we saw in it—all the good on our side, all the evil on the other—it was inevitable that the next generation should imagine it as an epic struggle like the Trojan War, fought by a generation that was braver, more patriotic, and more enduring than the next one could ever be.

Nostalgia and sentimentality are dangerous when they're about history. The people making this film will have to look out for memory's soft distortions. And avoid the windy words—*heroism, endurance, determination. Honor* and *celebrate*, too. If I'm going to be involved in this project, I don't want it to turn into a Veterans Day parade.

Just before Christmas Ken and Lynn reported again. The script is in process; they expect to have the first three parts in a draft by February or March, and the last two in April. So we're accelerating again. A rough cut will be ready by this time next year. I don't know what a rough cut is—or anything else about making a film, for that matter.

Scripts of the first two (not three) parts arrive on schedule, and at the end of March 2004 the World War Two Film Project advisors gather again in New York for two long days of hard work. We talk a lot about the home front: women, for instance— what roles they played in the war, who enlisted (I didn't know any girls from Minneapolis who signed up), what kinds of jobs they got in munitions factories, and how much the war and the new jobs and movement of people freed them from their parents' rules. And rationing—and the black market that was the criminal side of the war. And the way the army reported to families that their sons were dead. And we probe at particulars: Did that event really happen *then*? Were there *no* black sailors in combat jobs? What were the camps for Japanese-Americans really like? We are like a painter with a huge bare canvas, covering it with color, one brushstroke at a time.

At breakfast in the hotel dining room I read in the *Times* about the dead in Iraq. There are 592 of them now—such a small number, compared with the Americans who died in our war. But our guys are long gone, decayed into history; these young men (and women—the roadside bombs don't discriminate) were alive when our board first met a year ago, and now they're dead, and the *Times* puts them in a list: a marine PFC from Houston, a master sergeant from New York. There'll be more listed tomorrow. And the next day.

Episode three comes in the mail in August. It's mostly about D-Day—a truth-telling account, as far as I can see, though I worry a little about the tone here and there. It's the war-correspondents, I think; most of them have a streak of the cheerleader in them. We'll be better off if we stick to the stories the old soldiers tell: they may lack style, but they sound like the truth. And check the numbers: the historians I consult disagree on how many Allied troops died on the Normandy beaches.

That week, while we worked on the scripts, a mob ambushed and killed four civilian workers in Falluja, dragged the bodies through the streets, and hung two of them from a bridge. A few miles away five American soldiers were killed when a roadside bomb destroyed their armored personnel carrier.

With the first three scripts done, the Burns people went back into their caves (that's the way I imagined them) to do whatever it is that filmmakers do next, and we on the board returned to our lives. I took my wife, Liz, to London for Christmas, and in February (it's 2005 now) we spent a week in Barbados.

It was restful back in our usual life; I had no reason to think about my war for a while. I could just be a retired professor again. But I couldn't, because the country's other war, the struggle to occupy Iraq, went on, declaring its disastrous course in London newspapers and on the American television broadcasts that reached us down in Holetown. Because that war was present, our country's conduct in the Second World War was present, too, as a model of how war could honorably be practiced—how to declare it, fight it, and terminate it (though there was the bomb there at the end—that was a problem). Still you could say that our part of that war was played by the rules. Set against that example, Bush's war was an unruly scrimmage.

Walpole, New Hampshire, a little town (or maybe it's a village, or even a hamlet), is a sort of Burns enclave. We meet there at the end of June 2005. The place doesn't seem to be organized to be a town; the houses stand around randomly among the hills and pastures, as though they'd been tossed from a great shovel; there don't seem to be any street corners, not proper right-angled ones. There's a restaurant on what would be Main Street (if there were a main street), and a church hall, and out beyond what would be the edge of town is an inn where the board will stay. It seems a funny place to go to put a war together. I'm ill at ease in New England; it seems small and untidy, and the hills are too close together. But that's just Minnesota talking.

Every morning and afternoon we all sit in a room in the church hall while an episode is shown. There seem to be more members of the Burns army here than there were at our New York meetings—young men and women in jeans, mostly. I wonder if they just stay up here all the time, waiting for Ken and Lynn to need them.

Our job is different this time. Before, when we were working on written texts, it was just another editing job. But now the visual and aural form exists, and we're tuning it—questioning the accuracy of details, noting repetitions, trying to hear the soundtrack as a version of war, tightening the whole thing up. I sit at a table with a yellow legal pad and watch for problems and write them down, noting the date and time of each.

June 27:

10:37: what the film calls marine fighter-planes are actually TBDs.

11:08: we claim more dead Japanese pilots than planes shot down. Not every dead airman is a pilot.

2:50: the "British bombers" are American B-17s.

3:10: the image of a little boy in a soldier's helmet appears for the second time.

June 28:

9:45: shot of a swastika flag repeated.

3:20: "It was the heavies." But they're medium bombers.

June 29:

10:02: we call kamikaze pilots "volunteers." Not all of them were.

2:30: "the momentum problem." I'm referring to the Battle of the Bulge, but I'm no longer sure what I meant.

June 30:

9:10: that's a *Marine* pilot. (I'm surprised how jealous I am of the Marine Corps's reputation.)

11:45: The music at the end is the longest continuous stretch of slow sad music in the film. Is this the tone we want here? After all we *won*.

Across the top of the last page of my notes I have written: "A Great Act Five."

This has been the first screening. As the images moved on the screen, and the soundtrack thundered and whispered and sang, the thing we've been doing has come alive. Here are the men and women whose words I've been reading, the ordinary people who are witnesses to our war. These are the places they fought in—the fighting is still going on as I watch—and here are the machines they fought with—the bombers, the carriers, the tanks, the guns. It isn't history that I'm watching, exactly, not what happened in the past, but what it felt like to be there while it was happening.

Watching the rough cut, I learn a lot about the war I was in. That may seem paradoxical, after all I was there. But old soldiers will understand what I mean. You don't really see a war when you're in it; you're too busy doing your job or just keeping your head down to look around much, and anyway the view from a foxhole or the turret of a tank or a battleship is restricted. It isn't much better in the air, where I fought my war: there's always a lot of smoke around, and ground fire, and the other planes to watch out for, and your plane to fly. And besides, where you are in a war is only a small piece of the whole vast action. What I saw in the Second World War was mainly the southern end of a small island south of Kyushu. As I watched the rough cut, I begin to learn—no, to *experience*—what the rest of the war had been like. Looked like. Sounded like. Felt like. The real texture of it all. And not only the men who fought. Wives and mothers and children are in the film, too, and tell their stories, and I learn something about what it was like to wait, to work, to suffer, to grieve.

I needn't have worried about the big words in the prospectus; there are no celebrations here, and no heroes. Brave men, yes, and brave women, too, and one very brave ten-year-old girl. But not the glorified kind of brave—no Sergeant York charging the German machine-guns; no Audie Murphy on the roof of his burning tank, driving the enemy back; no Pappy Boyington over Rabaul daring the Japanese to come up and fight him. Almost no generals—though I was pleased to see General

MacArthur make a brief inglorious appearance escaping from Corregidor. No politicians making speeches. No official spokesman saying what he wished were true. No vanity, no boasting of brave deeds. Just men and women remembering their war.

Members of my generation will recognize themselves here, I think, and relive what they did sixty-odd years ago; and those old veterans we all know, who were there but never talked about it, will find their voices. And all those generations who are too young to remember will learn some of the real truths of war, the truths you don't learn from the newspapers and the evening news, and by the end of the film they'll understand a little what happens in the lives of human beings like themselves when they are caught up in the great machine of war.

At the end of the last screening I get up to go back to the inn to pack. But I stop at the door and turn back toward the crowded room. This final moment seems to require something more, a closing speech by a supporting player, like Fortinbras at the end of *Hamlet* or Edgar in *King Lear*. What I say is addressed mostly to the young people present; Ken and Lynn don't need my praise. I tell them they have created a huge original work of art. Ken has called it an epic poem; but you could also call it a more-than-Wagnerian opera, or a fourteen-hour-long symphony, or a fourteen-act tragedy. Tragedy is best. War is always a tragedy for those who endure it, the victors as well as the defeated. But, whatever you call it, the Burns crew should be proud of the work they've done.

Yet I go home depressed about war. Maybe that's because of the way the other war is going. While we were watching and talking up there in Walpole, some twenty young men—army special operations troops and Navy SEALS—were dying in the mountains of Afghanistan. I read their story on the train, how four members of a SEAL unit were dropped behind enemy lines to search for a Taliban leader and were sighted and pinned down. And how one of them, a navy lieutenant named Michael Murphy, climbed a bare ridge, exposing himself to hostile fire, because that was the only place where he could get a radio call out for help. How he made the call and was killed. And how the help came, a helicopter with sixteen guys in it, and how it was shot down, and they all died.

That's how courage expresses itself in a bad war, I think; in self-sacrifice. Brave men fall on live grenades to save their mates (a marine corporal named Jason Dunham had done that the year before), or walk into enemy fire, like Lt. Murphy, because there's nothing else to do. It's in the good wars—no, not *good*, the just and necessary wars—that they turn their courage toward the enemy, move forward, and make the other guys die. While we were up there at Walpole, President Bush explained to the country that the daily sacrifice of American lives "is worth it."

A week later Ken, Lynn, and Geoff Ward, the scriptwriter on the project, write to say how pleased they are with what the Walpole meeting accomplished. "We came away," they say, "with a sense that this film is saying things about the War and about war itself that need to be said, and that our country needs to hear." That's a crucial perception; the thrust of the film has changed, from the story of one historical war to "war itself." I've felt it, and they feel it—a weight, an obligation beyond what we intended when we set out.

Ordinary life resumes. And ordinary death. That fall I fly to London for the funeral of an old friend (if you're old enough to have served in The War you go to a lot of funerals). There's another screening when I return, this one in a New York television studio. The film has continued to grow; there are now seven parts. We watch for four-and-a-half days, morning and afternoon. The summarizing letter from Ken and his colleagues when it's over has the same startled, excited quality that the

July letter had: "The film seems to have accrued an emotional force and power we did not fully appreciate until the screening," they write. That's true; it's not only getting longer, it's deeper than we imagined it would be.

As I rattle home on the Trenton local I'm still unhappy with the ending—the slow sad music that goes on and on, and the haunted veterans who speak what the music says—that for them the war hasn't ended. I write to Lynn, protesting that it wasn't that way, that in America the war ended in jubilation. It was the last time in our century that American people would welcome their soldiers home with celebrations. Our film should show that. But I'm wrong; I'm still thinking about the film we set out to make, not the one we made. The subject of our film is "war itself," not what came after. Or it carries "war itself" on past the armistice into the lives of men who couldn't turn their backs on it but went on living in its world of loss and grief, the men who "had a bad war."

The wars in Iraq and Afghanistan go on, too. On the first day of our October meeting the *Times* announces that the roster of American dead has reached two thousand men and women. And the dying goes on: eight more on our second day, seven on the third. In Afghanistan 203 men have been killed since operations began there in 2001.

The Burns brigade goes back to its cave to complete the final phase, and the board members go back into their lives. In mid-March 2006 Lynn writes a relaxed retrospective letter; work on the film isn't quite complete, it isn't in the can, but it's whole and coherent, and she likes it. And the board's job is done. I feel a sort of deflation; I've served in Ken's war longer than I served in my own, and now I'm a civilian again.

On the day of Lynn's letter the *Times* reports that eighty-five Iraqis have been executed by Iraqis. Many were tortured—

torture is now a part of the war discourse. The total of Iraqi dead is said to have reached six figures, though nobody knows for sure. President Bush says, "We will not lose our nerve."

September 29, 2006: Navy Petty Officer Michael Monsoor is with a sniper team in Ramadi, Iraq. An insurgent throws a grenade among them. Monsoor throws himself on the grenade, protecting his comrades, and is killed when it explodes.

December 4, 2006: Private Ross McGinnis is riding through a Baghdad neighborhood in a Humvee. Someone throws a grenade into the gunner's hatch. McGinnis could jump out, but instead he drops the hatch and covers the grenade with his body, absorbing the fragments in the explosion. He dies instantly. The rest of the crew survives.

A few months later advance DVD copies of *The War* arrive. Mine won't play on my ancient television set, but I don't mind. I was there at the birth; I saw it grow.

In May the Public Broadcasting Station executives meet in Dallas. I make a short speech to them about the film, trying to describe what it does, and the change that occurred in the making of it. The speech ends something like this:

> The working title of this film was "The History of the Second World War," but the film you are going to see is called simply "The War," as though the events of 1939–45 were only one episode in the huge, continuous war that is always being fought somewhere, always has been and always will be, humankind being what it is, and this film is simply a sample of the nature of all war—past, present, and the one that is coming. It's in no sense a polemical work, either for or against war; you don't have to preach when you have authentic images and true testimony to tell the story. It simply shows what war is like.

The War was premiered in the United States on September 23, 2007. Nothing notable happened in Iraq or Afghanistan that day, though the next day the papers reported that the total dead American service men and women had now reached 3,787.

October 22, 2007: Lieutenant Michael Murphy, the man who died on that bare Afghan ridge, is awarded the Medal of Honor.

✳

First published in the Sewanee Review *(Spring 2010).*

In the Whirl and Muddle of War

Sometime in the late 1920s, Horace Pippin, a Black American veteran of World War I, began to write his memories of his war. It must have been difficult: Pippin was not a writer and was not very well educated. Even the physical act of writing was hard for him, for his right hand and arm had been crippled by a sniper's bullet and he could scarcely hold a pen. Yet he tried several drafts of a war narrative before he gave the writing up and turned to drawing and finally to painting. That, too, was a struggle; he had to hold the brush in his crippled right hand and guide its movements with his left. He worked at one painting for three years, giving it, he reckoned, a hundred coats of paint. It was called *The End of the War: Starting Home*, and it hangs now in the Philadelphia Museum of Art—a strange and powerful image of the violence that he remembered.

What is it that so drives a man, over such obstacles, to record his vision of war? In Pippin's case it could not have been any thought of an audience or a market; there was no one who would read his words, and no one who was likely to buy a painting of war by a handicapped amateur in West Chester, Pennsylvania. Clearly the force that moved him came from within: his memory and his imagination were engaged in a private, urgent transaction.

There have probably always been men who have felt the need that Pippin felt, to record in words and images the wars they have fought. Not all old soldiers, of course—everybody knows some old man, an uncle or a grandfather or the man down the street, who "would never talk about it"—but a great many of them. The books they wrote fill shelf after shelf of any research library, and an archive like the Imperial War Museum in London has hundreds of unpublished narratives, often handwritten and carefully hand-bound, each the story of one man's war. As new wars are fought, new records are written. You don't have to be a scholar of the war in Vietnam to know that it produced many accounts of the fighting there; and no doubt right now, as I write, some solitary Russian soldier, stuck in Afghanistan in a war he doesn't want to fight, is putting it all down, not for posterity but out of a private need.

I have been reading a lot of such documents lately for a course that I teach on the literature of war. Not novels (the great war novels are familiar enough) and not the writings of generals (the records of command are their own subject), but personal narratives of ordinary soldiers: veterans of the Napoleonic Wars, Civil War volunteers, Victorian troops out on the edges of the empire, junior officers and enlisted men in both world wars, Vietnam grunts. It is a literature not much studied, or even read, except by military historians and war buffs. And yet, when you think about it, war is one subject that has been continuous in the human story. The history of the world is the history of war, one old soldier remarked; and who can refute him?

The wars that this literature records have been very different in terrain and technology, but the accounts have one quality in common: each is the witness of a single separate consciousness, one tense young man in the whirl and muddle of war. The stories that these men tell are small-scale—a man doesn't see much of the world looking down a gun barrel—and the reality that they render is particular and physical. They have nothing to say about strategy or about why men fight, only about how they fight, and where, and how they die. They make war vivid, but they don't make it familiar; indeed, one motive for writing seems to be to record how unfamiliar war is, how grotesque its ordinary scenes are. Pvt. Elisha Stockwell describes the regimental camp after the Civil War battle at Corinth, Mississippi:

> When I got back to camp, they had everything loaded on the wagon, and we moved on to the east side of town where they were fetching the wounded. They were laying them in rows with just room to walk between. They had tents for those that were the worst off, and where they were amputating arms and legs. There was a wash-out back of one tent that had a wagon load of arms and legs. The legs had the shoes and stockings on them.

War consists of actions that no man would otherwise perform—like cutting off a wagonload of arms and legs—and it takes place in anti-landscapes that are contradictions of the landscapes that human beings live in. When the poet Wilfred Owen tried to describe the "No Man's Land" of World War I in a letter to his mother, he could do so only in images that have nothing to do with actual scenery:

> It is like the eternal place of gnashing of teeth; the Slough of Despond could be contained in one of its crater-holes; the fires of Sodom and Gomorrah could not light a candle to it—to find the way to Babylon the Fallen.
>
> It is pock-marked like a body of foulest disease and its odour is the breath of cancer. . . .
>
> No Man's Land under snow is like the face of the moon:

chaotic, crater-ridden, uninhabitable, awful, the abode of madness.

War turns the natural world into evil, indescribable spaces, and everything in it into broken, useless, unidentifiable rubbish—including human beings. Reading soldiers' accounts of Shiloh or Waterloo, Ladysmith or the Argonne or Hue, one sees with estranged eyes. These lives are not ours, and never could be; and these places are like nothing that we can know in our ordinary worlds.

There seem to be two quite different needs that produce war writing: the need to report and the need to remember. The reporting instinct operates as war happens, and appears in letters and diaries that at their best realize the unimaginable. But such documents are more than simply narratives of military actions; they are also the stories of young men's lives, as much about growing up as about fighting. Wars force their participants to confront the questions that life will put to them anyway, but not so bluntly: Am I a leader? Am I a coward? When required to act, will I fail? You don't have to label this challenge the test of manhood (a term that is not in much favor these days); call it instead the test of maturity, or of selfhood. War confronts the soldier with a challenge in terms that make success or failure nakedly clear.

Life back home doesn't often do that. So the letters and diaries that soldiers write are also report cards; they say that this young man has taken the test, and has passed. Here, as an example, is a passage from an artilleryman's letter after the British defeat by the Zulus at Isandlwana:

> We played well on them with the two guns, and the infantry
> fought well, cutting roads through them. We held the field
> from half past eleven in the morning until three o'clock in

the day. We killed twelve thousand Zulus, but they were too strong for us. They came right around us, and massacred every one; there are only twelve left to tell the tale. Out of sixty-five artillery only four remain, and I am one of the four.

The message of this letter is more than simply "I'm still alive." It is: "I was tested; I fought; I survived."

Letters and diaries of soldiers record what is memorable as it happens. But there is another, more complex kind of personal narrative: the remembered war that persists in the mind through a lifetime. Shakespeare imagined such a memory in a veteran of Agincourt: "Old men forget; yet all shall be forgot, / But he'll remember, with advantages / What feats he did that day." That was no doubt true of Agincourt, and it has been true of battle memories since then. Elisha Stockwell was fifteen when he joined the Wisconsin Volunteers in 1861, and eighty-one when he wrote his recollections. William Manchester's *Goodbye, Darkness: A Memoir of the Pacific War* was written in the late 1970s, more than thirty years after the Pacific war that is its subject. Roald Dahl waited nearly forty years to write *Going Solo*, his memoir of the RAF during World War II.

Not all war narratives have waited so long to get written, but the best appeared well after the events that they narrate. Most of the memoirs of World War I that we still read—Robert Graves's autobiography *Good-bye to All That*, Siegfried Sassoon's *Memoirs of an Infantry Officer*, Edmund Blunden's *Undertones of War*—didn't appear until the end of the 1920s. And the same seems to be true of our most recent war: Philip Caputo's *A Rumor of War* was published twelve years after he left Vietnam, and Robert Mason's *Chickenhawk*, about Vietnam in the 1960s, was written in the 80s.

In these remembered wars, the time that separates events from writing about them is clearly an important shaping factor. The experiences are those of a young self. Young men at war feel life and death with an intensity that is beyond peacetime emotions. They know comradeship, a closeness to other men that ordinary life frequently does not provide. They see their friends die, and they feel grief that is different from what they have known before, back home, where folks die naturally, and mostly old. They feel fear, and the exhilaration of fear overcome. And they are changed.

It is their older selves, the selves on the other side of those deep changes, who write the memoirs. They look back on themselves when young, when innocent, as though on another life, and the questions that they ask of memory are different from those that a young man asks. The usual narrative questions are posed: What happened there? What happened then? But behind them are deeper questions: Who was I then? What happened to me? Who did I become? Courage is no longer the challenge; that question has been answered. Truth of being is what matters now. So William Manchester, after thirty years of not remembering his life as a young marine, returned to the islands to rediscover it and wrote a fine book about it. "This, then," he writes at the end of his narrative, "was the life I knew, where death sought me, during which I was transformed from a cheeky youth to a troubled man who, for over thirty years, repressed what he could not bear to remember." By then he *had* remembered, and had come to terms with his memories.

To perceive the changes that war has made in a man requires the passage of time and the establishment of distance from the remembered self, and it is not surprising that most war memoirs come late, that memory dawdles and delays. There have been cases, though, when the sense of change came quickly, when a man looked back over a short life and saw extreme changes in himself and wrote his story while he could. Richard Hillary wrote *The Last Enemy*, the best memoir of the Battle of Britain, while the war was still going on. Hillary was shot down over the Channel during the air battle and was horribly burned. Surgeons gave him a new face—a grotesque mask of the handsome young man he had been—and even new hands, and it was that damaged man, distanced from his old self by his disfigurement, who recorded his change and then returned to the flying that he knew would kill him (as it did).

But Hillary was an exception, a man of unusual perception and unusual sufferings who understood at once what had happened to him and could write well enough to put his understanding into immediate words. For most men, understanding comes more slowly; and imagination must wait upon memory to reveal itself.

When it does, it picks its favorites, who are not usually war's favorites. Heroes are, by and large, no good for war memoirs; they stand too close to the center of war's values, and whether they mean to or not they act out the mottoes on the flags and the slogans on the posters. What suits memory best, it seems, is a war life lived close to the action, but at some distance from the values, lived by a man who is by nature or circumstances an outsider, who can be a witness as well as a soldier. Robert Graves was an untidy, undisciplined officer; William Manchester went into battle against orders; Robert Mason was a helicopter pilot who was grounded for psychological reasons; Tim O'Brien (who wrote *If I Die in a Combat Zone, Box Me Up and Ship Me Home*) tried to go AWOL; Keith Douglas (who wrote the best memoir of the North African tank war, *Alamein to Zem Zem*) was a disobedient and eccentric officer.

Memory likes the man without medals. Mason should have gotten the Distinguished Flying Cross, but didn't; Graves was awarded no medals, nor was Douglas; Pippin deserved a Purple Heart, but had to wait twenty years to get it; Sassoon had a Military Cross, but threw it into the sea (an act, you might argue, that freed him to write one of the great war memoirs). Memory also has its style, a plain way of telling that leaves the emotions and the drama to emerge from events themselves. I've just come upon an American memoir of World War I that I hadn't known existed: *Toward the Flame* by Hervey Allen, who later became briefly famous for writing *Anthony Adverse*. In the preface to his memoir, Allen sets down what amounts to the esthetic of war writing:

> I have tried to reproduce in words my experience in France during the great war. There is no plot, no climax, no happy ending to this book. It is a narrative, plain, unvarnished, without heroics, and true. It is what I saw as nearly as memory has preserved it, and I have set it down as a picture of war with no comment.

The memoirs that matter are like that: plain, unvarnished, and unheroic. They move like the infantry, upon the surface of the earth, or in the unsubstantial air above it; they record weather and dirt, cold and heat, as well as violence and fighting. Rifleman Harris, whose *Recollections* is a classic of Napoleonic War memoirs, has a vivid description of the retreat to La Coruña, Spain, through bitter winter weather in which he recalls "passing a man and woman lying clasped in each other's arms, and dying in the snow. I knew them both; but it was impossible to help them. They belonged to the Rifles, and were man and wife." You get the same mix of death and weather in the best of the Vietnam memoirs, but there the weather is heat and rain, and the dead women are Vietnamese—different details, but the same particularity. That's what memoirs are made of: in the ontology of war remembered, there are no abstractions.

Wars sometimes unite societies while they're being fought, but in the end they change and divide them. A generation that has lived through a war is different from one that hasn't; and within a war generation, those who fought stand apart from those who didn't. One war generation will be separated from another by the character of its wars: there are good wars and bad ones. My generation, the one that fought in World War II, was fortunate; we lived through a war that took so many lives nobody can calculate the casualties (20 million military dead is a possible number, plus nobody knows how many civilians), and yet came out at the end feeling that we were still entirely virtuous and our enemies entirely evil. My children's generation, which lived through Vietnam, had a tougher time, and I'm sorry for them.

But beneath the differences of cause and justification, wars are wars for the men who fight in them. Philip Caputo writes in his prologue to *A Rumor of War*: "I have found myself wishing that I had been the veteran of a conventional war, with dramatic campaigns and historic battles for subject matter instead of a monotonous succession of ambushes and fire-fights." That seems to me to reveal a failure of imagination, or of historical sense, in an otherwise very sensitive writer. For there are no such conventional wars, and if Caputo had read Sgt. Lamb on the American Revolution, Pvt. Wheeler's letters from Waterloo, John Beatty on Chickamauga in the Civil War, or Robert Graves on the Somme, and by reading their stories had fought with them, he would know that the dramatic campaigns and the historic battles take place in the history books and not in the memories of soldiers.

War is unfamiliar, unimaginable, insane, appalling. But it is a primal human activity, and a memorable one, and men who have fought—not all of them, but some—have had a deep need to record what they saw and felt. Not for us, I think, but for themselves, to say, like the ubiquitous Kilroy, *I was there.* And perhaps also to try to order the meaningless incoherence that a war seems to be to those who fight, not misrepresenting the disorder but putting down plainly what happened and so, perhaps, finding themselves. We readers are not the primary audience of such memories; but we may listen in, and listening we may learn something of what the world of war, so unfamiliar and yet, alas, so human, is like, to those who for a time inhabit it, and are changed by it. And who remember it.

*

First published in the New York Times Book Review, *July 31, 1988.*

War Stories

MYTHS OF WORLD WAR II

Americans like anniversaries—even anniversaries of disasters. So here we are, fifty years after Pearl Harbor, "celebrating" our nation's greatest naval catastrophe. It seems an appropriate occasion to look back not at what happened on that Sunday morning in Honolulu but at the whole war—and at what remains of it in our minds, in our imaginations. For some of us, of my own generation, there are memories, as untrustworthy as most memories are; for all of us there is a Myth, the story of the war that we have composed over the years—out of recollection, and other people's narratives, and various memorable images. A myth in this sense is not a falsehood: it is simply the sum of what we have come to accept as the truth, the order that we have made of past events so that we can understand them, and live with them. We have such myths in our minds of many passages of history: we share, for example, a story of the First World War, though none of us was there. We've put it together out of novels and poems and movies; and since we have all read the same war-books and seen the same films about that war, the story is much the same for all of us. And we all believe that story to be the truth about what happened from 1914 to 1918.

Our myth of the Second World War is less clear, less vivid, and less interesting than our myth of WWI. The story seems sprawling and unfocused—it was such a huge war—and lacking in high drama and moral complexity. Perhaps for those reasons it has not generated the classic literary expressions of it: fifty years after the armistice there is no canon. You can test the truth of that proposition very simply: make a quick list of the great war-books of the WWI; then list the great ones of WWII. I'll give odds that every reader has a list of at least four or five WWI classics, and they are all the same: *All Quiet on the Western Front*, *A Farewell to Arms*, *Good-bye to All That*, Wilfred Owen's poems, Sassoon's *Memoirs of an Infantry Officer*. Lists for WWII will be shorter, more various, and less confidently made: *The Naked and the Dead*, perhaps; maybe *From Here to Eternity* (though it isn't strictly speaking a war-novel), or Richard Hillary's *The Last Enemy*, and perhaps a few poems by Keith Douglas and Henry Reed. There are some books, and there is a story of sorts; but the Myth exists only as a bare moral fable: Good confronted Evil, and Good won. It has not found canonical form, and we are still more deeply moved by the writing of the other, earlier war.

Why should that be true? I offer some reflections on that question, and some tentative answers.

In many, perhaps most, national histories in this century there has been a point of violent change, a fracturing crisis of faith in the values that had until that point propelled and unified the nation. It has come at different times in different countries: in Germany in the 1920s, in Spain in the 30s; in the Soviet Union it happened in 1917, and is happening again now. In England that fracture came during the First World War when the people, especially the fighting troops, lost confidence in their cause and their leaders, and became disillusioned and bitter. English writing about the war fed on that disillusionment; it is the great theme of that literature, which is the most brilliant and the most moving of any writing about war in our time.

The First World War wasn't like that for Americans. There was no great disillusionment and no change in national feelings about leaders and values. And there were virtually no significant American war-writers—only Hemingway, who stayed in Europe after the war, and so tuned in to the English and Continental mood.

The Second World War didn't disillusion us either. We entered the war as a nation for a combination of patriotic and humane motives—more patriotic in the Pacific, more humane in Europe—and we came out of it nearly four years later still feeling good about ourselves, still calling it a "Good War," though by then sixty million human beings had died in it. (Or so one calculation has it. But statistics on total deaths in the war are untrustworthy and conflicting. There were simply too many dead, in too many places, to count. And no doubt in many cases no survivors to do the counting.)

No, we Americans had to wait until Vietnam for our national disillusionment. In terms of social shock and imaginative response, WWII wasn't a shock to the national system: nothing changed, nobody lost faith, we simply went, and then we came back. There is a sense, though, in which disillusionment *was* a part of the experience: not as a present loss, but as an inherited attitude. When Robert Sherwood remarked in 1948 that the second war was "the first in American history in which the general disillusionment preceded the firing of the first shot,"[1] I think this is what he meant—that the English war-writing of the First War was already there, in the general consciousness, as a way of comprehending war. The young participants knew, before they heard a shot fired in anger, that this was not going to be a heroic war, that one should expect nothing, use no Big

1. I found this useful quotation in Paul Fussell's excellent anthology *The Norton Book of War* (1991).

Words to describe one's feelings, and distrust the big words that one's elders used. It was all there in Owen and Sassoon.

Disillusionment is not quite the right term for that attitude; *irony* is better. Irony was a serum with which Americans had been inoculated against the disillusionment that had shaken England in the First War; it made us immune to that embittering virus. Perhaps it also made us immune to the deepest feelings about the war, those feelings from which the greatest writing comes. It is striking that the best-selling books about the war in this country during the war years were mainly comic or sardonic ones: *See Here, Private Hargrove*, or *The Feather Merchants*, or *Shore Leave*, or *Love at First Flight*. We were sardonic in our wartime gestures, too. Above the bar in an officers' club on some Pacific island—was it Eniwetok?—there was an enormous brassiere, mounted on a board like a stuffed tarpon, with below it this slogan burned into the wood: REMEMBER PEARL OLSON. A typical military joke, you might say; we Americans are a wise-cracking people. But a joke about Pearl Harbor, in wartime? It seems to me significant that servicemen's irony had reached that far, that soon.

The status of disillusionment is one difference between the two wars that might begin to explain the differences in their literatures and myths. There are, of course, other differences—historical ones—that are important. For example, numbers: How many men were involved? How many died? We think of the second war as vastly larger than the first, and in geographical terms it was; but in terms of total combatants there was not much difference (though here again the figures are slippery). The Allies in both wars mobilized forces in the forty millions; the Central Powers in the First War and the Axis in the second managed just about half that number. But, though the numbers of troops were roughly the same, the deaths were strikingly different. The Allies in the Second War lost more than double their losses in the first—eleven million against about five million, while Axis forces lost less than half as many as the Central Powers did—five million in the Second War, twelve million in the first.

The figures for the United States make a separate point, since American troops were only in action in the First War during the last few months of the fighting. In that war we mobilized four million men and lost fifty-three thousand—roughly the same number as in Korea and Vietnam. In the Second War more than sixteen million Americans were under arms, and more than a quarter of a million died.

Can anything useful be inferred from all those big numbers? Do they have necessary imaginative consequences? In the case of American war-writing they obviously do: Americans simply weren't there long enough the first time to feel the war as the French, British, Germans, and Russians did. To come to the truth about the First World War seems to have required the experience of suffering over time. But for the rest, when casualties are in the millions, does it matter to the imagination how *many* millions? I can't see that it does, unless one argues that sheer mass, the dead in their mountainous heaps, will turn the imagination from heroism to bitterness and grief—or to silence.

What about the scale and range of fighting in World War II—the huge naval battles, the skies black with bombers, the vast invasions, all of Europe and the whole Western Pacific as battlefields? What about the Battle of Britain, Stalingrad, El Alamein, Guadalcanal, Midway, Okinawa? Surely those were epic conflicts, worthy of epic writing. But to my knowledge no epic was written; certainly none has been recognized as the canonical story of any of those battles.

Is it possible that the trouble with those battles as subjects for imaginations is that our side won? Perhaps it is too late, in our ironic century, to create an epic war-literature out of victories. It is certainly true that the war-books we still read about the First War have nothing to say about winning. The best-known novel of that war—*All Quiet*—was by a writer on the losing side, and its appeal was as strong in England and America as it was in Germany. Most of the memorable poems are not about either winning or losing, but about suffering, as though the question of who won in the end was simply not relevant, since in any case the men who fought would be losers.

Yeats said, in a famous passage in his *Oxford Book of Modern Verse*, that "passive suffering is not a theme for poetry." But he was wrong: in the First War passive suffering was the *only* theme. This was at least in part a consequence of the kind of war it was—a virtually stationary standoff in trenches that stretched from Switzerland to the North Sea. That meant that the dead remained with the living, as part of the landscape of war. Wilfred Owen wrote, in a letter to his mother, of experiencing the effect of those dead presences, "whose unburiable bodies sit outside the dug-outs all day, all night, the most execrable sights on earth. In poetry we call them the most glorious. But to sit with them all day, all night . . . and a week later to come back and find them still sitting there, in motionless groups, THAT is what saps the 'soldierly spirit'" (February 4, 1917).

So perhaps the mobility and range of the Second War, the constant moving on from one beach full of bodies to another, was an imaginative disadvantage; perhaps the execrable is a necessary part of a myth of war in our time. Perhaps it also helps when the killing and the dead are close up as well as constant in that landscape. Trench warfare had that advantage over the bombing of Berlin; so did the Trojan War. In general the more modern the war the more remote it has become. Of the most recent example, the Gulf war, the one image that most of us retain is a mechanically triggered film of an electronically directed missile on its way to destroy a bunker. No human being is visible in that image: it is machine against concrete. What kind of a myth can be made out of that?

A war in which one hundred thousand of the enemy died, remembered in a single inhuman image. Perhaps it is true that visual images have replaced the printed word in our culture, as the primary source of our conceptions of reality. Perhaps that brief film *is* our Myth of the War against Iraq. And, if that is true, then maybe we should be looking for the real canon of the Second War not in books, but in the visual arts.

I'd suggest that we look first at the work of Bill Mauldin, beyond any question the finest draughtsman of World War II. Mauldin created two G.I.'s, Willie and Joe, and in doing so created *all* G.I.'s, as Kipling is said to have created Tommy Atkins. They slouch across the title page of *Up Front*, his book of drawings, scruffy and unshaven, wearing fatigues that are like Salvation Army castoffs—two wry, skeptical, war-wise veterans, on their way from one dirty battle to the next. A few pages into the text we find them seated on the ground, digging foxholes. Willie is saying: "You'll get over it, Joe. I wuz gonna write a book exposin' the army after th' war myself." In another drawing Willie (or is it Joe?) shuffles along beside a column of captured German soldiers. It is raining, the Germans look defeated, Willie is gloomy, the whole war-world is wet and ruinous. The caption reads: "Fresh, spirited American troops, flushed with victory, are bringing in thousands of hungry, ragged, battle-weary prisoners . . . (News item)."

These two drawings are not simply about war: they are also about language. Willie and Joe speak a tough ironic soldiers' English; part of the joke in that first drawing is that we know Willie couldn't write a book, even though what he would have to say would be worth reading: he can only *be* the truth about the war. In the other example the visual image works with harsh irony against the official rhetoric of war in the quoted item. War isn't what *they* say: it's what *we* feel. Words can't be trusted; the truth is in the direct experience of the senses. The conclusion that follows from this is one that every old soldier knows to be true: only the men who were there know how it was. If you weren't there, shut up.

Bill Mauldin made the American G.I. imaginable and real. *Life* magazine did the same for war's landscapes; its influence on American imaginations during the war years cannot be exaggerated. Everybody looked at *Life*'s pictures (I don't think most folks read the prose), and from them got such notions as they had of what was going on in the war, what being a soldier or a sailor or a marine felt like, and how war was actually fought. From the war's beginning *Life*'s images were harshly realistic and full of death. There were images of prisoners being shot and bayonetted, of heaps of dead Chinese civilians after Japanese air raids, of a dead Russian mother with her still-living baby. *Life* brought the grim news of Pearl Harbor to American living rooms, and made the hideousness of war vividly clear in pictures of beaches littered with Japanese dead. There was only one restriction: in the first years of the war there were no pictures of *American* dead. That restriction was lifted in the summer of 1943, when the government apparently became convinced that American civilians weren't taking the war seriously enough. One of the first results of this liberation was the publication of George Strock's famous shot of Buna Beach, with three American soldiers lying at the water's edge—bloated, maggoty, sand-covered, very dead. Later there was a shocking sequence of a Japanese soldier actually burning to death in a napalm attack. You couldn't quite feel the same about combat after seeing those pictures. So maybe we *do* have our canonical versions of the Second War; we have simply been looking in the wrong places.[2]

There is another sense in which we may have been looking in the wrong places, which I can best approach via another theory. It is possible to think of every war as having a center of horror, a battlefield or a battle or a series of actions, or maybe a way of dying that is the focal point of its greatest suffering, its most terrible violence. In Napoleon's wars it was the retreat from Moscow; in the Crimea it was Balaclava if you were English, Sevastapol if you were Russian; in Korea it was the ambush at the Chosin Reservoir. In the First War the center was the Western Front: virtually all of the important, myth-making books and poems came from there. Nobody remembers any writing about Gallipoli, or Salonika, or about naval actions, and from the Italian front there is only *A Farewell to Arms*. What was and still is perceived as the worst realities of the war happened in France—on the Somme, at Verdun, in the mud at Passchendaele; our images of what that war was like, the war-story that we imagine and believe, comes from those terrible scenes.

The center of horror in the Second War was on no front at all. Instead it hovered over a number of places: Auschwitz and Buchenwald, Dresden, Tokyo, Hiroshima, Nagasaki. These are the scenes of the most pitiful aspect of modern war, the war fought against helpless civilians. A graph of the civilian dead in major wars in this century would surely be a steadily rising line, from the First War (the Belgians who died when the German army swept through their country, the English who were killed in Zeppelin and bomber raids), to the Spanish Civil War

2. On this point of *Life*'s treatment of the war, I am indebted to Jonathan Marwil's "How We Remember the Good War," *Chicago Tribune Magazine*, December 1, 1991.

(where the Germans at Guernica made the first systematic attack on a civilian population), to the people of Shanghai and Stalingrad in the Second War, the uncounted dead in Vietnam (where soldier and civilian were indistinguishable), to the bodies in Baghdad. The war against civilians is our century's most striking contribution to the methodology of war.

If this Theory of the Center of Horror is sound, then one might expect that the most powerful writing of the Second War would come not from the battlefields, but from scenes of civilian suffering. And so it has. There *is* a canon of strong and moving books about those places, which includes Eli Wiesel's *Night* (Auschwitz and Buchenwald), Primo Levi's *If This Is a Man* (Auschwitz), Kurt Vonnegut's *Slaughterhouse Five* (Dresden), the stories in Kenzaburo Oe's *The Crazy Iris* (Hiroshima)— and there are many others. From these books the element of fighting—which is the active potentially heroic side of war—is absent; they are pure suffering. The story that they tell should be at the center of our myth of the Second War.

That story, with its huge and pitiful numbers, has not been assimilated into the myth; and because it hasn't, the Second War can remain an undisillusioned narrative. For it is there among those helpless dead that the fracture ought to have occurred; the disillusionment with strategies and weapons and the judgments of leaders should have been felt by all of us there. But the truth of these annihilations reached us only gradually, after the war was over, almost as footnotes to the story; and the war against civilians remains a separate set of narratives, as though those fires had burned in some distant alternative world.

Still there was the war we remember, the ordinary war of armies against armies. Some eighty million men fought in that war: can't a canon of truth-telling books be gathered that would tell their story? Well, yes, I think it can; such books exist, though they are not of the profound and terrible kind that came out of the war against civilians. They are, rather, the most modest personal accounts, many of them written by people who never wrote another book. They tell ordinary war-stories in plain language, most of them—stories that could be multiplied by tens of thousands to express the experiences of the mass of indistinguishable individuals who filled the vast canvases of the war.

I'd suggest books like John F. Bassett's *War Journal of an Innocent Soldier*, the *Pacific War Diary* of James J. Fahey (who went back home to Waltham, Massachusetts, to spend the rest of his life as a garbage man), the slender English classic *Hugh Dormer's Diaries*, Keith Douglas's *Alamein to Zem Zem* (this one by a fine war-poet, but nonetheless a narrative of ordinary war), *Trial by Battle* by David Piper, and Yoshida Mitsuru's *Requiem for Battleship Yamato*. The story that these books together tell is not as intense or as disillusioned as the books that make up the First War's myth; indeed, one point that they make is that the fighting in the Second War didn't turn its participants to bitterness. They come as close, I think, as we will get to the story that will tell us how it was in World War II; though that story will be incomplete, and so in the end a misrepresentation of the whole reality, without those other millions, the people who died in the scorched cities and the crematory ovens, in our Good War.

*

First published in the Sewanee Review *(Winter 1992).*

A Critic Looks at War

I must begin with a disclaimer. My subject is war, but I don't write as a military historian. I think of myself as a critic; what interests me are words—words about war, and the narrative they compose—and the nonverbal gestures of the other arts, too, when their subject is war. You could say that I'm interested in the rhetoric of war, not the actions, in the war stories that men tell, not the wars they fight. From words about war we learn all that most of us will ever know about war: its incidents and its values, its causes and its consequences, what happens in war, and what it feels like if you're where the shooting is. From these words, we construct the imagined narrative that we all share, that is collectively our culture's myth of war. We all have that myth in our heads: it's one of the primal themes of human imaginings.

My subject here is the wars of the twentieth century as we imagine them: how those stories gathered and took shape and lodged in our brains, where they came from, what they tell us, and what they *don't* tell us about war. And how they change.

I'll begin, in the manner of an epigraph, with war words that didn't originate in our century but are nonetheless a part of war as we imagine it—a fine rhetorical passage from *Othello* in which the general, tormented and deceived, says goodbye to his profession:

> O! now, for ever
> Farewell the tranquil mind; farewell content!
> Farewell the plumed troop and the big wars
> That make ambition virtue! O, farewell!
> Farewell the neighing steed, and the shrill trump,
> The spirit-stirring drum, the ear-piercing fife,
> The royal banner, and all the quality,
> Pride, pomp and circumstance of glorious war!
> And, O you mortal engines, whose rude throats
> The immortal Jove's dread clamours counterfeit,
> Farewell! Othello's occupation's gone!

Here is the great tradition of war: as a splendid spectacle, glorious, spirit stirring, full of pride, pomp, and circumstance, a calling worthy of the Good Soldier who fights in it. It's an image of war that is rather like the Trooping of the Colors, only it's real (as the thundering cannons remind us at the end).

Othello's war—so full of value terms and high romantic images—is the dominant rhetoric of war in Western culture from Shakespeare's time into the twentieth century. Not the only rhetoric—Wellington didn't talk like that and neither did Sherman, nor the common soldiers who remembered the old campaigns. But literary folks who hadn't fought in a war did: Wordsworth did, and Tennyson, and Henty and Kipling. And so did the schoolboys who read them. Glorious War was a theme that gripped the imaginations of writers and artists and lured young men into bright uniforms, and into battle.

In the twentieth century, all that changed. Or so we say. To look at that change, we must begin with the First World War, not simply because it takes chronological precedence but because it was the great transforming datum of the time: the twentieth century begins in 1914.

The received view of the First World War is that it was so terrible that it obliterated the idea of Glorious War entirely from human imagination. After the fighting on the Western Front, there could be no more pride, pomp, and circumstance, no more heroics, no more Rupert Brookes. From that point on, war stories would have to be told without Big Words: *anti*-rhetoric would be the only style.

Two of the most quoted passages in the literature of the First World War are about rhetorical inversion. One is the preface that Wilfred Owen drafted for the volume of poems he didn't live to see published:

> This book is not about heroes. English Poetry is not yet fit to speak of them. Nor is it about deeds, or lands, nor anything about glory, honour, might, majesty, dominion, or power, except War. Above all I am not concerned with Poetry. My subject is War, and the pity of War. The Poetry is in the Pity.

A series of rhetorical prohibitions: all Othello's big-value words must be stripped from the language of war; only one abstraction remains, the antithesis of the old war rhetoric—*Pity*.

The other passage is from Ernest Hemingway's *A Farewell to Arms*. Frederick Henry, Hemingway's alter ego in the novel, is on the Italian Front with his ambulance unit. He's talking with an Italian friend, who says: "What has been done this summer cannot have been in vain." Henry thinks:

> I did not say anything. I was always embarrassed by the words sacred, glorious, and sacrifice and the expression in vain. We had heard them, sometimes standing in the rain almost out of earshot, so that only the shouted words came through, and had read them, on proclamations that were slapped up by billposters over other proclamations, now for a long time, and I had seen nothing sacred, and the things that were

glorious had no glory and the sacrifices were like the stock-yards at Chicago if nothing was done with the meat except to bury it. There were many words you could not stand to hear and finally only the names of places had dignity. Certain numbers were the same way and certain dates and these with the names of places were all you could say and have them mean anything. Abstract words such as glory, honor, courage, or hallow were obscene beside the concrete names of villages, the numbers of roads, the names of rivers, the numbers of regiments and the dates.

Two famous statements against the high rhetoric of war; but we mustn't make the mistake of taking them to be statements about *war*. These are *writers'* statements; they're about what the war these two writers saw did to the inherited language of war. They aren't polemical; they don't say: "Don't make war!" or "Never again!" They say: "Don't *talk* about war in those big, empty words; don't invest it with your old, hollow values." But war itself remains, as solid and as real as earth.

What was it about the First World War that made the purgation of war's rhetoric so necessary? Was it really radically different from what wars had been in the past? Was it worse than earlier wars had been? Worse than the wars with Napoleon? Worse than the Crimea? Worse than the Civil War? Or was it simply a matter of *scale*? Or was it perhaps that this was the first Big War (to use Othello's value term) to be fought mainly by amateurs, including substantial numbers of the educated middle class, and so was Europe's first *literate* war, in which many of the men who fought were capable of writing down their witness to the truth of what they had seen and suffered?

All of those were factors, I think: the First World War *was* worse, it *was* bigger, and it certainly *was* recorded. There was one other factor that changed war from 1914 to 1918: by an accident in the pace of scientific development, the First World War was fought at a time when modern weaponry was more advanced defensively than offensively (though of course the generals had not registered that fact). It was a war in which it was easier to kill and be killed than it was to win, a stationary war of trenches, barbed wire, and corpses.

Let's pause for a moment over that point. Technology alters reality: we'd all accept that obvious proposition. The reality of war becomes a different reality when it includes machine guns that can fire six hundred rounds a minute and are accurate over two thousand yards, and artillery that can shell positions miles away, and poison gas. Farewell the plumed troop when such weapons come to war: farewell the cavalry charge, the sabers and the lances; farewell heroism. Farewell the Good Soldier who draws his pistol and cries: "Follow me!" as he goes over the top to glory. In this war, such individual acts won't make any difference: machines, and the capacity of nations to produce machines, will determine who wins.

In that machine-war, fundamental things change. Soldiers become sufferers, *victims* of their war and not *agents* in it. The First World War that we have in our heads tells us that. We know the huge casualty figures and how those men died—blown to bits by guns they couldn't see, drowned in flooded shell holes, choked by gas, incinerated by liquid fire; we know that in the spring offensive of 1917 French troops marched to the front baaing like sheep because they were going to the slaughter and knew it, and that fifty French divisions mutinied; we know that soldiers in every army sank into states that army doctors called shellshock, a condition that wasn't physiological at all but rather a mental breakdown brought on by helpless fear; we know that trench suicides and self-inflicted wounds were common and that the troops observed such acts without judgment.

We *know* that war: it's in the books we read, the memoirs

and novels and poems from which we have constructed the war in our heads. We know the antirhetorical way those stories are told, the plain language and the bitter, ironic tone that acknowledges and plays on the dissonance between imagined war and the real thing. That war story is our Myth of the war: it expresses what we all agree the First World War *means*.

It's an entirely dark, entirely terrible story. And it's true: men who were there did those things, felt those emotions, wrote those words. It's what the Western Front must have been like—a place for which Owen's one abstraction, pity, is the only possible response.

But it isn't the whole story; there are other stories from that war that the Myth excludes. To find them, you'll have to dig into books that aren't in the canon, and that none of us reads. Look, for example, into a thick gray volume from the United States Government Printing Office titled *Medal of Honor Recipients, 1863–1973*. An interesting book: a list of all the individuals who have been awarded our nation's highest medal for military valor, with their citations. But it's more than just a list: these stories amount to a history of heroism in America and how it has changed over the century and a half that the medal has been awarded.

Here are the men whose behavior is, you might say, rhetorical. Look at the first couple of citations in the World War One section:

ADKINSON, JOSEPH B., who all alone charged an enemy machine gun position across fifty yards of open ground, kicked the gun from the parapet into the enemy trench, and took the three gunners prisoner at the point of the bayonet.

ALLEX, JAKE, another one-man army, who attacked a machine gun nest, killing five of the enemy with his bayonet, and when it broke using the butt of his rifle, and taking fifteen prisoners.

You won't have heard of Joe Adkinson or Jake Allex, but you may have heard the last name in the First World War list: YORK, ALVIN C. He led seven men against a machine-gun position and captured four officers, 128 men, and several guns. If you're my age, you'll remember that this story was made into a popular movie, with Gary Cooper as Sergeant York.

Three war stories, but all the same action—the classic act of heroism on the Western Front, one man or a few men armed with handheld weapons attacking a machine gun: *old* war attacking *new* war, the Good Soldier attacking the victim-maker. And note how the weapons used regress back through the history of warfare: a firearm, a stabbing weapon, a club—back to the most primitive form of man-to-man killing. As though the generals, or whoever determines who wins the Medal of Honor, were telling the world that war had not changed, that individuals could still win battles by their courage. In the citations, the old Big Words are used without irony: "greatest intrepidity," "took command," "fearlessly leading," "heroic feat." Othello would have been at ease in their company.

One hundred eighteen Americans were awarded Medals of Honor in the First World War. These men saw the same war that Owen and Hemingway saw; but it's a *different* war in their stories, *not* a war of victims but a war in which individual acts of courage are performed, and recognized, rewarded, praised without irony. Yet they're not in the story of their war that we tell ourselves. Why not? What's *wrong* with these actions as World War war stories? Well, you could say that they're the wrong acts to illustrate an antiwar Myth: they're neither disenchanted nor bitter; they're not *victim* stories.

To tell those stories properly, you'd have to use the Big Words that our myth of the war disallows; and you'd have to believe them. You can't do that without violating the Myth, and so Sergeant Adkinson, Corporal Allex, and Sergeant York simply aren't there in our version of the war—neither the men nor their actions nor the words that would describe them.

In the received view of history, the decades of the 1920s and 30s, the years *entre deux guerres*, were a time when the Dark Myth of the First World War took form—a pacifist, antiwar, antiromance time. Or so, at first glance, it seems to have been. In the late 1920s and early 30s, virtually all of the canonical warbooks of the First World War were published: *Good-Bye to All That, Memoirs of an Infantry Officer*, the *Poems of Wilfred Owen, A Farewell to Arms*, and, most definitive of all, *All Quiet on the Western Front*, a novel that sold millions of copies and was translated into dozens of languages, and then, just in case anyone missed it, was made into a memorable film and shown around the world. I don't suppose any other single war story in history has had such an influence on the way people think and feel about a war, and about War.

And the books weren't the only signs of that pacifist spirit. At Oxford in February 1933, the students of the Oxford Union passed a famous resolution: that the members of the Union would not fight for King and Country. Millions of Britons joined the Peace Pledge Union and pledged never to fight. And in the US, on college campuses, students organized the Veterans of Future Wars. You'd be justified in thinking that, for that twenty-year period, the Western world (minus the Germans in the 1930s) was entirely and passionately disenchanted with war and its values.

But look again, look elsewhere. The war had barely ended when the war memorials began to be built. And they were *rhetorical* memorials. Walk down Whitehall in London and look at the tall stone monument that is Lutyens's Cenotaph and read its rhetorical inscription: "The Glorious Dead." Stop at the tomb of the Unknown Warrior at Westminster Abbey and read its message:

BENEATH THIS STONE RESTS THE BODY

OF A BRITISH WARRIOR

UNKNOWN BY NAME OR RANK

BROUGHT FROM FRANCE TO LIE AMONG

THE MOST ILLUSTRIOUS OF THE LAND

AND BURIED HERE ON ARMISTICE DAY

11 NOV: 1920, IN THE PRESENCE OF

HIS   MAJESTY   KING   GEORGE   V

HIS MINISTERS OF STATE

THE CHIEFS OF HIS FORCES

AND A VAST CONCOURSE OF THE NATION

THUS ARE COMMEMORATED THE MANY

MULTITUDES WHO DURING THE GREAT

WAR OF 1914-1918 GAVE THE MOST THAT

MAN CAN GIVE LIFE ITSELF

FOR GOD

FOR KING AND COUNTRY

FOR LOVED ONES HOME AND EMPIRE

FOR THE SACRED CAUSE OF JUSTICE AND

THE FREEDOM OF THE WORLD

THEY BURIED HIM AMONG THE KINGS BECAUSE HE

HAD DONE GOOD TOWARD GOD AND TOWARD

HIS HOUSE

That, surely, is the ultimate rhetorician's case for war. Look at the Tomb of the Unknown Soldier at Arlington Cemetery. Look beyond the words at the rhetorical gestures of the monuments themselves: at the Menin Gate at Ypres, with its arrogant Brit-

ish lion couchant across the top, at Lutyens's great triumphal-
ist pile of bricks at Thiepval on the Somme. Certainly there is
plenty of high war rhetoric in the official world of monuments;
the nations needed those piles of stone to deny that ten million
men had died in vain (that phrase that Hemingway so hated).

But if you look again, more closely, you will find an element
of subversion in all those rhetorical gestures. The Cenotaph is
an empty tomb; the corpses in the Abbey and Arlington Cemetery are *nobodies'* bodies. And while the outside of the Menin
Gate displays its victorious lion, the walls on the inside are in-
scribed with the names of fifty-six thousand British soldiers
killed in the Ypres salient (only up to August 1917) whose bodies
were never found. Lutyens's monument is the same: it bears the
names of the missing on the Somme, seventy-three thousand
of them.

In these memorial instances, the words and gestures of romantic valued war occur but are subverted by the reality, by
one corpse unnamed or fifty thousand lost: not *famed*, not
glorious—just *dead*. That, I think, is what really happened in
imaginations after the First World War: rhetoric met reality,
and the dream of war became ironic. But that doesn't mean that
the dream was erased from human minds: irony doesn't annihilate meaning, it only makes you uncomfortable with it.

The romance of war lived on, between the wars, in monuments and ceremonies (Armistice Day, for example, when
at eleven a.m. in every American schoolroom students stood
silent for two minutes), and in less elevated forms in the day-
dreams of popular culture. If you went to the movies during
the 1930s and early 40s, as I did, you might see *All Quiet on the
Western Front* and come away appalled by war; but you might
see *The Fighting 69th* or *Sergeant York* and go home thinking
that war was a brave and glorious business. Or you might see
one of the great films of war in the air—*Hell's Angels* or *Dawn*

Patrol—and find the war-dream there: war as adventure, war as chivalry, doomed heroes and sacrificial gestures. I still remember the last scene of *Dawn Patrol*: Richard Barthelmess takes off in the half-darkness, his long white scarf trailing in the slipstream, to fly another man's patrol, and die.

The point is that as the 1930s came to an end—after two decades of dark mythmaking, after the poems of Owen and Rosenberg, the memoirs of Graves and Blunden, the novels of Ford and Remarque—romantic, glorious war was still alive. If it was denied in "high" culture, it turned up in popular culture. It was even present in the Navy's quartermaster's store. When I was commissioned as a Marine pilot in 1944 and went to draw my flight gear, I was handed a long white silk scarf, just like Richard Barthelmess's. Someone in Procurement must have seen *Dawn Patrol* and thought he knew what a pilot should wear when he took off on his last, doomed mission.

Many historians consider the Second World War simply a continuation of the First, after a twenty-year remission; and in some ways that is certainly true. On war monuments, for example, 1939–45 or 1941–45 is likely to be a footnote carved on a stone that was erected to commemorate 1914–18. But in terms of the rhetoric of war, there was a difference. War could still seem an adventure, or even a crusade (General Eisenhower could call his war-book *Crusade in Europe* without apparent irony); but the First World War *had* been fought. A generation of young men had gone to that war drunk with the excitement of it all (not *all* of them—one must go easy with the generalizations— but *most*). War had detoxified them, and they had returned to write down their hangovers. The young men of the next generation would not go to *their* war quite so innocently, or use the Big Words so easily, or return so bitterly, but would manage to combine in their remembrances the Rightness of their war and its Reality, its rhetoric and its antirhetoric.

There is one war memorial that seems to me to express that mixed response with particular clarity. The Marine Corps Memorial at Arlington isn't really a World War II monument, but it *seems* to be, since its figures are a reproduction in bronze on a gigantic scale of one of the most famous of World War II photographs, the raising of the flag on Mount Suribachi, Iwo Jima. That group of huge bronze men is a perfect example of what I mean by rhetoric in visual terms: five men in combat gear, five times as big as life, straining to raise a symbol of the Good War over an Evil Place.

That's the rhetoric. The antirhetoric is less obviously visible; you have to approach the monument to see, carved around the plinth, the names and dates of Marine Corps battles since the Corps' beginning in the American Revolution: the French Naval War, 1798–1801; Tripoli, 1801–1805; Haiti, 1915–1934; Belleau Wood, 1918; and on to my own place in the story, Okinawa, 1945. When I first saw the memorial, I resisted the huge rhetorical gesture of the cast figures, but I was moved by the battle names and dates. I think I understood, then, Hemingway's point about language: it isn't simply that the rhetoric sounds hollow; it's that the names *are* more powerful than the gestures.

But in this memorial both the gesture *and* the names are true; or, together, they tell a dissonant truth about that war, its rhetoric and its reality. Perhaps that dissonance is why my generation didn't find it easy to write about our war. We had been in a "Big War"—the biggest in history. We had gone to it thinking it was necessary, maybe even a Good war, and most of us had returned still believing that it had been a parable of moral struggle that had ended with the victory of Good over Evil. But it hadn't ended in a romantic way; there had been no last great battle. Instead, it had ended with two terrible victim stories: the liberation of the death camps, and the bombing of Hiroshima and Nagasaki.

The immediate literary response to the war was curiously muted. Nobody wrote a big, best-selling novel (though Norman Mailer tried); nobody was acknowledged as the great war poet; there was no canon. The best war-novels in those first postwar years were small ironic ones—Tom Heggen's *Mr. Roberts* (1946); John Horne Burns's *The Gallery* (1947); Herman Wouk's *The Caine Mutiny* (1951)—novels that were not about heroes or heroic deeds, but about ironists and losers. Ten years after VJ Day, there was still no defining memoir. As for films, there were a few ambitious but dreadful attempts at heroic war (John Wayne in *Sands of Iwo Jima*, for example), but very few good ones. To my mind, the best wartime film was one that had no visible war in it all but got the mood exactly right: *Casablanca*, a film that is all irony, and that ends (we could all recite the scene) with an ironic American saloonkeeper and an ironic French cop walking off through the fog to fight ironically against the Nazis. And yet, there is no doubt in the film that the war is a struggle between Good and Evil; only this war will be fought with a wise, unrhetorical weariness, as befits a *Second* World War.

After the Big Wars, the Little Wars: Korea, a war without either a rhetoric or an antirhetoric, without a story, without even a memorial until the 1990s, when one was finally built. A forgotten war, in which, nevertheless, some 37,000 American troops died. It's not that *nobody* wrote about that war; there were a few excellent memoirs, quite a few not-so-good poems, James Salter's novel *The Hunters* (1956), James Michener's *The Bridges at Toko-Ri* (1953). But the Korean War still has not reached American imaginations, and never will. It wasn't *really* a war, we think; it was only a police action. And it didn't properly *end*; it simply stopped. Maybe that's why it never acquired a meaning, never became a Myth (except maybe in reruns of *M*A*S*H*).

And then Vietnam: our bitterest war, our war of disenchantment; the war we shouldn't have fought; the war we lost. In some ways, it was like Korea: a war fought on an Asian peninsula against communist forces, in which 58,000 Americans died. And four million Vietnamese. (In Korea, the number was around two million.) We tend to forget those enemy casualties (most of them civilians). We shouldn't, though, because civilians have been the huge majority of all dead in all of the twentieth century's wars. At the beginning of the century, 15 percent of war casualties were civilians; at the century's end, the figure was about 90 percent—another aspect of the way in which, over the century, war became victim-war.

In other ways, Vietnam was a very different war, a unique American catastrophe. Its difference was partly demographic. This was a war that middle-class American boys stayed away from. Anyone who was a college teacher in the late 1960s and early 70s will remember how few students left school for military service, and what desperate steps they took to avoid being drafted. (To some extent, this was also true of Korea, but not nearly as much.) The people who went were mainly the poor: inner-city blacks, white country boys out of work, Hispanics. Some of these young men were sharp observers and vivid writers; vivid talkers, too (this was the first war to produce extensive oral histories); but they came from outside the usual middle-class writers' sphere, and the stories they told, and the way they told them, were different. Their narratives have their own tone and their own rhetoric; they are often foul mouthed, stoned, demotic, with their own special characters—tunnel rats, dinks, short-timers, crazies—and their own resonant place-names, which are not the names of battles won: Khe Sanh, Hue, My Lai.

The Myth of the Vietnam War began very early and grew as the war went on. Its constituent elements were the brutal violence "in country," as the G.I.s said—especially against civilians, against women and children (students demonstrated in the streets of our cities, chanting "Hey, hey, LBJ, how many kids did you kill today?"); the confusion—inevitable in war but intensified in Vietnam by the jungle terrain and the local guerrilla tactics; and the troops—younger than any previous American army, ill-trained, uncertain of their cause, in-country for only 365 days, *whatever* happened in the fighting. And one other element: having fought this brutal war as they were told to fight it, they came home to be spat on and called murderers by their fellow Americans. And to weep, go berserk, and fill the mental wards of army hospitals. It's a myth with no heroic ending.

That's the Myth of the Vietnam War that we all have in our heads. Like the First World War's myth, it is a story of victims; but unlike the first war, it lacks the saving element of tragedy. To be a victim in a *Little* War that is wrong is, somehow, diminishing, degrading. The spit still clings to it.

In the stories Vietnam veterans tell, aggressive individual courage is not courage: it's either stupidity or ignorance. Here's a passage from one of the oral histories—from a Specialist 5 called "Light Bulb" Bryant. Light Bulb is remembering a white guy from Oklahoma who said the reason he volunteered was to go to Vietnam and kill Gooks.

> It was a week after he had just gotten there that we got into any action. He was just itching to get into some. We went out and got pinned down by machine guns. They were on our right flank. He saw where the machine-gun nest was, and he tried to do the John Wayne thing. He got up, trying to circle around the machine-gun nest. Charge the machine gun. And never made it. Whoever was firing saw him move and turned the machine gun on him.

You must hear in that story a parody of those First War heroes—Adkinson and Allex and York. What was heroism for them is "the John Wayne thing" for old Light Bulb: a dumb joke at some Okie's expense.

Yet there *were* men who behaved heroically in Vietnam, and the Army recognized their heroism and awarded them Medals of Honor—240 of them (compared to 118 in World War I). Yes, but what *kind* of heroism? The Medal's establishing definition was that it should be given for "conspicuous bravery or self-sacrifice." We saw what conspicuous bravery meant in the First World War Medal of Honor stories (and saw it mocked by a Vietnam grunt). Vietnam citations tell a different story. Let me quote a sentence or two from among the first dozen citations in the official list.

ANDERSON, JAMES JR.: Suddenly, an enemy grenade landed in the midst of the marines and rolled alongside Pfc. Anderson's head. Unhesitatingly and with complete disregard for his personal safety he reached out, grasped the grenade, pulled it to his chest and curled around it as it went off.

ANDERSON, RICHARD A.: Observing an enemy grenade between himself and another marine, L/Cpl. Anderson immediately rolled over and covered the lethal weapon with his body, absorbing the full effects of the detonation.

ANDERSON, WEBSTER: Seeing an enemy grenade land within the gun pit near a wounded member of his gun crew, Sfc. Anderson, heedless of his own safety, seized the grenade and attempted to throw it over the parapet to save his men. As the grenade was thrown it exploded.

Three examples of the same act, and I'm still in the Andersons. Go on to AUSTIN, BACA, BALLARD, and you'll find it repeated. Six Medals of Honor, all for acts of self-immolation to save other men. And if you look at other citations, the ones that don't involve live grenades, you'll find that virtually all of them have an element of that same selfless concern for other men, the wounded, and the helpless. Clearly, the meaning of heroism has changed: but *why*? Had these soldiers lost their belief in the value of aggressive acts of courage against the enemy? Was it that in this war that couldn't be won such acts were meaningless? God knows, what these men did was courageous, but it was different. What they displayed was *victim* courage.

That's a view of the Vietnam War that the memorial wall in Washington confirms: a monument entirely without rhetoric, neither Big Words nor upward-thrusting stone: only names. It's a war memorial that says nothing except *dead, dead, dead*— 58,000 times.

After the Little Wars, the Littler Wars: Grenada, Gulf I, Bosnia, Kosovo, Somalia, and a lot more, in one place or another. For wars go on all the time, thirty or forty are being fought right now, as I write: territorial wars, civil wars, tribal wars, police actions, local campaigns of ethnic or religious cleansing, genocides. No memorable words have come out of those conflicts that I know of, no memoirs or novels or poems that fix that war story in the canon of war.

Only once in all those battles have extraordinary acts of individual courage occurred, and been recorded, that seem at first glance to merit a place among the classic accounts of Good Soldier courage. They happened in Mogadishu on October 3, 1993, in an operation that had begun as just another UN police action, but got out of hand and became a war. Snipers had pinned down an infantry unit in town, and a helicopter hovered above, directing fire, until it was shot down and crashed in the street. A soldier ran out from cover to try to save the men inside, and was shot dead. Another soldier tried, and he too was killed. Two men in action, extraordinarily brave—the kind of personal courage that merits the Medal of Honor. But it isn't really a Good Soldier story of the traditional kind: these soldiers were not attacking the enemy; they were sacrificing their own lives for unknown comrades. Their story belongs with all those Vietnam stories; they did the only thing they could do in a stalled and incoherent situation—they died. Both men got their Medals of Honor, but old Light Bulb would have called what they did "the John Wayne thing."

The century of Big Wars and Good Soldiers may be said to have ended there, on the Mogadishu street. We have come, I think, to the end of the Big Words and the brave gestures and the tall stone monuments. There will be no more aggressive heroic war stories: Othello's occupation's gone.

Looking back over the past hundred years, we can see the two World Wars looming like two great mountains on a plain, dominating the century. As those wars have receded into history, they have become more than historical events: they have become Myth—two Big Wars, one Bad and one Good, together embodying the whole of what human beings can do to one another and to their world when they take arms against each other. It is a truth about *us*—one pole of our bipolar humanity.

The Little Wars are forgotten, but the two World Wars are still with us, in our imaginations. The First War has passed entirely out of living memory now. There are no more eyewitnesses to tell us how it was at Belleau Wood and the Somme; there can be no more memoirs. But the war is still alive in our heads; novelists write novels about it, playwrights write plays, filmmakers make films. The Second War, twenty years younger, still exists in the memories of my generation, and even now, more than sixty years after the last shot was fired, a memoir occasionally appears. And novels, and films. Those wars, so far in the past now, are still the wars that move and stir us; they are *our* wars.

It's easy enough to see why the imaginations of novelists and filmmakers are drawn to the Big Wars. Artists have always needed epic materials to create art: Homer needed Troy; Tolstoy and Hardy needed the wars with Napoleon; Stephen Crane needed the Civil War.

And what about *us*, the readers and moviegoers who make those images of the Big Wars best sellers and box-office hits? What draws us to those fearful images? Why do we seem to need Big Wars and Good Soldiers in our heads? You could reply at once that war is history and that our motive for seeking out its stories is simply our desire to know the past. But war is *more* than history: war is a drama of destruction acted out in fire, the most extreme violence that human beings can suffer and inflict, the terrible dark side of existence.

War is also the human struggle against human enemies— against Evil, Fear, Death itself. Against those enemies men have sometimes performed acts of great courage and self-sacrifice, qualities that we recognize as humanly valuable, even as we hate the wars that bring them into being. War stories are witnesses to such acts, not performed by heroes but by people like us. Like Wilfred Owen, we may pity our fellow humans, pitched into war scenes of such extremity, but like Hemingway we must recognize the dignity of what they do. They are ourselves, elsewhere; and their actions are our extreme possibilities.

It seems unlikely that memorable war stories will come out of the wars that the Western world is fighting in our new century; the invasions of Iraq and Afghanistan go on and on, but they're Little Wars, in which one side has most of the technological weapons and the other side has most of the casualties. They're victim wars, for both sides; there will be no new myths, no epics there. If that is so, our writers and artists and filmmakers, the myth-tellers of our culture, will surely continue to return to the two World Wars, and we will return with them to learn again that war is terrible, and yet that in war men may act beyond the limits of their ordinary natures. We will need both of the war myths that the twentieth century has bequeathed to us from its Big Wars—the myth of violence and the myth of courage—to tell our war stories in the twenty-first century.

Epilogue: September 2016

That prediction about the "Little Wars" in Iraq and Afghanistan was wrong, as I should have known. They were and are peculiar wars—undeclared and unfinished, aimless and endless and small-scale, wars in which everyone who's not in uniform may be an enemy, and men die one at a time. Still, memorable war stories have come out of those conflicts, books like Phil Klay's *Redeployment*, Chris Kyle's *American Sniper*, and Roy Scranton's *War Porn*. These accounts lack the narrative sweep and the vast scale of their Great War predecessors, and they have their own bitter tone, their own rough grunt-vernacular. But what they tell us has the ring of truth; we need them, along with all the other stories of our bellicose past. Together, these stories demonstrate one incontrovertible truth: there will always be wars, and the men who fight them will feel the need to bear witness to what *their* war was like.

Hardy and the Battle-God

When critics write about modern war poets, they rarely mention Thomas Hardy. In our time, just past the end of a century of wars, we take *war poet* to mean a poet who was a soldier first, who learned about war by fighting before he wrote about it. The war poems that matter are the ones that take us where we have never been, into the unimaginable experience of war. "What was it like?" we ask the poet. "Tell us, you've been there, you know."

Hardy had not been there. He never saw a war, never heard a bullet fired in anger; the battlefields he visited were scenes of long-ago fighting, no longer battle scenes but memorials. And yet he wrote one great war epic, one poem that makes a war that was a century past when Hardy wrote about it as immediate and real as the Dorset earth. *The Dynasts* is a monstrous great poetic drama of nineteen acts and one-hundred-thirty-one scenes, too long ever to be acted straight through, too long some would say even to be read. Still, there it is, the real thing, the nearest English poetry has ever come to a war epic, and the last one we shall ever have, because it was written in the last decade in English history in which a war epic was possible.

Hardy never saw a war, but he nevertheless had a war in his

head, derived not from direct experience but from memories and fictions. We all have such imagined wars, before we have real ones, wars made of whatever our time and culture give us. From such accidental stuff, we construct our private myths of war. Hardy tells us in various places what the sources of his war-in-the-head were. Here is his account of his earliest reading, from *The Life and Work*:

> About this time his mother gave him Dryden's *Virgil*, Johnson's *Rasselas*, and *Paul and Virginia*. He also found in a closet *A History of the Wars*—a periodical in loose numbers of the war with Napoleon, which his grandfather had subscribed to at the time, having been himself a volunteer. The torn pages of these contemporary numbers with their melodramatic prints of serried ranks, crossed bayonets, huge knapsacks, and dead bodies, were the first to set him on the train of ideas that led to *The Trumpet-Major* and *The Dynasts*.[1]

Later, when he was sixteen or so, he read the *Iliad* to teach himself Greek, and found another epic war.

Virgil, Homer, and a history of the Napoleonic Wars—these are predictable texts from which a bookish Dorset boy in the mid-nineteenth century might create his version of essential war. But war did not appear to him only in books. Dorchester was a garrison town, and Hardy saw a good deal of the resident troops; they walked the streets of Dorchester and Weymouth, they turned up in the neighboring villages (as Sergeant Troy does in *Far From the Madding Crowd*), they departed for distant wars, and some of them returned. Hardy remembered

---

1. Thomas Hardy, *The Life and Work of Thomas Hardy*, ed. Michael Millgate (1984), 21.

their picturesque uniforms well enough half a century later to write a precise footnote to *The Dynasts* describing the look of the Hussars' sling-jackets. And he remembered their stories.

From the town's old men he heard other stories. Hardy's grandfather was dead before his grandson was born, but other local volunteers in the wars against Napoleon were still alive, still telling their tales. Hardy acknowledged his debt to these parish historians in his preface to *The Trumpet-Major*:

> The external incidents which direct [this novel's] course are mostly an unexaggerated reproduction of the recollections of old persons well known to the author in childhood, but now long dead, who were eye-witnesses of those scenes.[2]

These old persons appear in Hardy's novels and stories (Grandfer Cantle in *The Return of the Native* is one), and in early narrative poems like "Valenciennes," "San Sebastian," and "The Alarm," poems that carry dedication lines connecting them to actual local soldiers: "S. C. (Pensioner)," "Sergeant M— (Pensioner)," and "One of the Writer's Family who was a Volunteer during the War with Napoleon" (that would be Hardy's grandfather)[3]—as though he felt a need to demonstrate that the war in his head was not altogether an invented one.

One other source was neither written nor spoken. All his life, Hardy saw history as a story recorded on and below the surface of the earth—a story that preexisted its articulation in words. The earthworks of his countryside, the Roman stones of his town's walls, the bones and shards he found buried in his garden were all silent witnesses from the Dorset past. History lay

2. *The Trumpet Major*, p. v.
3. *The Complete Poetical Works of Thomas Hardy*, ed. Samuel Hynes, 5 vols. (1982–95), I: 24, 27, 46.

everywhere around him. He makes this point in *The Trumpet-Major* preface:

> Down to the middle of this century, and later, there were not wanting, in the neighbourhood of the places more or less clearly indicated herein, casual relics of the circumstances amid which the action moves—our preparations for defence against the threatened invasion of England by Buonaparte. An outhouse door riddled with bullet-holes, which had been extemporized by a solitary man as a target for firelock practice when the landing was hourly expected, a heap of bricks and clods on a beacon-hill, which had formed the chimney and walls of the hut occupied by the beacon-keeper, worm-eaten shafts and iron heads of pikes for the use of those who had no better weapons, ridges on the down thrown up during the encampment, fragments of volunteer uniform, and other such lingering remains, brought to my imagination in early childhood the state of affairs at the date of the war more vividly than volumes of history could have done.

From these silent texts Hardy got a sense not so much of the present reality of war as of its pastness: these are the materials of a myth of war such as an imaginative boy might conceive who has come along too late for the reality.

The sources of Hardy's war-in-the-head are a disparate set from which to make war poetry: Homer and Dorset village historians, a popular Victorian picture-paper, the *Aeneid*, Greek gods, an outhouse door, a green sling-jacket. But among these oddments there is material enough for the themes of war: the violence and the brutality, the dead bodies and the grieving families; and the romance—the brave uniforms and the drums and the roaring cannons; and the grandeur—great armies flowing like rivers, cities burning, dynasties falling. To understand

Hardy's wars one must begin back there in the boy's imagination, with the old men's memories and the bullet-riddled door, and with the sense of a long-past time when war was epic.

The dream of a possible epic war poem runs through Hardy's journal of his novel writing years, vague at first (but always *epic*), coming at last to form and focus as *The Dynasts*. The first such entry in *The Life and Work* is this one, from June 1875: "Mem: a Ballad of the Hundred Days. Then another of Moscow. Others of earlier campaigns—forming altogether an Iliad of Europe from 1789 to 1815." If you turn back a page from this passage you will find that it comes just after Hardy had visited the Chelsea Hospital in London, where army pensioners lived; the date was the sixtieth anniversary of Waterloo, and he went there to talk with survivors of the battle—seeking out, on this memorial occasion, the company of the old men and their memories.

Two years later, Hardy had discarded the ballad form for drama:

> Consider a grand drama, based on the wars with Napoleon, or some one campaign, (but not as Shakespeare's historical dramas). It might be called "Napoleon," or "Josephine," or by some other person's name.

A few years after that he was thinking of it again as a drama, and the following year again as a ballad, this time "A Homeric Ballad, in which Napoleon is a sort of Achilles," uncertain, here in the 1870s and 80s, as to what form could best contain his vast ambitions. But the ambitions were never in doubt: he would write a poem of the greatest events in modern European history, an epic poem on an epic scale.

In epic poems the forces that move the universe and rule the wills of men appear as gods and goddesses; but in a modern epic set in nineteenth-century historical reality such figures obviously would not do. How could the century's shaping philosophical ideas—determinism, upward evolution, the world-as-will—be given forms and voices? Hardy worried away at this problem in his journal, beginning with this 1881 note:

> Mode for a historical Drama. Action mostly automatic; reflex movement, etc. Not the result of what is called *motive*, though always ostensibly so, even to the actors' own consciousness. Apply an enlargement of these theories to, say, "The Hundred Days"!

No form for the ideas there yet; five years later there was:

> The human race to be shown as one great network or tissue, which quivers in every part when one point is shaken, like a spider's web if touched. Abstract realisms to be in the form of Spirits, Spectral figures, &c.

These reflections do not come close to describing the actual philosophical machinery of *The Dynasts*; what they show is that in the 1880s Hardy was thinking of his war epic not only as modern history, but also as an expression of modern—that is, late-Victorian—ideas of the forces that move history and impel human actions, and the ironic relations between what those forces do and what men think they themselves do.

But before Hardy set himself to write his war epic, he was drawn to address a different war. England's quarrel with the Boers was scarcely epic—anti-epic if anything, a small discreditable colonial action fought with less than complete support from the folks at home, and with little glory in the field. The last Victorian war: why should Hardy have bothered to write a set of poems about it? Not out of patriotic enthusiasm, surely; Hardy was not a man who got excited about current events. Nor from public spiritedness; he was a reluctant public man (and wisely so, to judge from the few occasions when he attempted public poetry). Perhaps the answer is simply that he used the Boer War as a sort of trial run for his big intended war poem, an opportunity to test the elements of the war-in-the-head against a real one, to see which of those elements he could use, and how.

He began, characteristically, in Wessex: three poems about the embarkation of local troops from Southampton (he rode his bicycle all the way from Dorchester to watch them depart). Then a poem about a local man killed in the war, and later another local remembering how he killed an enemy. Writing the poems, he stressed their localness. "Drummer Hodge" was first printed with this headnote: "One of the Drummers killed was a native of a village near Casterbridge"; "The Man He Killed" is staged like a play—"SCENE: The settle of the Fox Inn, Stagfoot Lane . . . The speaker (a returned soldier), and his friends, natives of the hamlet" (Stagfoot Lane was Hardy's name for a hamlet north of Puddletown in Dorset). These poems are like the stories the old soldiers of his youth told, war stories, but rooted in Wessex.

Of the war matter in Hardy's head, he found he could use the local scene well enough, and the local dead, too—a drummer, one enemy soldier, husbands mourned by their wives, a cloud of souls of the dead, sweeping home over Portland Bill. And irony, as in poor dead Hodge, thrown uncoffined into his grave under the wheeling southern constellations, so small a corpse, so vast and strange the universe. What he could not do, yet, was *war*: he might call his set of poems "War Poems," but the customary trappings of war are all missing; no arms, no armies, no generals, no cannons, no drums, no trumpets, no battles, no cavalry charges, no deeds of personal heroism, no victories, no defeats. The last Victorian war poems of the last Victorian war have no war in them.

Hardy himself noted another Victorian element the poems lack: in a December 1900 letter to his friend Florence Henniker, accompanying a copy of his "Song of the Soldiers' Wives and Sweethearts," he wrote: "My Soldiers' Wives' Song finishes up my war effusions, of which I am happy to say that not a single one is Jingo or Imperial—a fatal defect according to the judgment of the British majority at present, I dare say."[4] He was right on both points: his poems were not jingoistic; and they did offend the British public, or at least that portion that wrote (and read) the London *Daily Chronicle*. Two days before Christmas 1899, Hardy published "A Christmas Ghost-Story," one of his "War Poems," in the *Westminster Gazette*. In it a British soldier, dead and buried in South Africa like Drummer Hodge, asks:

> "I would know
> By whom and when the All-Earth-gladdening Law
> Of Peace, brought in by that Man Crucified,
> Was ruled to be inept, and set aside?
> And what of logic or of truth appears
> In tacking 'Anno Domini' to the years?
> Near twenty-hundred liveried thus have hied
> But tarries yet the Cause for which He died."

The *Daily Chronicle* responded on 25 December with a Christmas Day leader. "Mr. Thomas Hardy," the *Chronicle* wrote,

> has pictured the soul of a dead soldier in Natal contemplating the battlefield, and wondering where is that peace on earth which is the Christian ideal of Christmastide. A fine conception, but we fear that soldier is Mr. Hardy's soldier,

---

4. *Collected Letters of Thomas Hardy*, ed. Richard Little Purdy and Michael Millgate, 7 vols. (1978–88), 2: 277.

and not one of the Dublin Fusiliers who cried amidst the storm of bullets at Tugela, "Let us make a name for ourselves!" Here is another ideal which conflicts, alas! with the sublime message we celebrate today. . . .[5]

There is a basic Victorian conflict in this quarrel: between the idea of moral evolution upward—Hardy called it "evolutionary meliorism"—and its opposite, which we might call Victorian Belligerence, or perhaps Romantic Imperialism. Hardy's Boer War poems contain a good deal of the former theme; it's a Victorian commonplace, and we may take it as a sign of this delusion's popularity that even the usually pessimistic Hardy shared it. It is present as a question at the end of "Departure," one of the embarkation poems:

> When shall the saner softer polities
> Whereof we dream, have play in each proud land
> And patriotism, grown Godlike, scorn to stand
> Bondslave to realms, but circle earth and seas?

And more assertively in the closing poem of the group, "The Sick Battlegod," which ends:

> Let men rejoice, let men deplore,
> The lurid Deity of heretofore
> Succumbs to one of saner nod;
> The Battle-God is god no more.

That pacific view of war stayed in his mind through the decade that followed; you find it, for example, in his 1913 poem, "His Country," with its one-world, antiwar marginal gloss: "He trav-

5. *London Daily Chronicle*, 25 December 1899, quoted in *Complete Poetical Works of Thomas Hardy*, I: 368.

els southward, and looks around; / and cannot discover the boundary / of his native country; / or where his duties to his fellow-creatures end; / nor who are his enemies."

The other view, the Victorian-Belligerent one, was also in Hardy's mind, as he confessed in a letter to Mrs. Henniker:

> I constantly deplore the fact that "civilized" nations have not learnt some more excellent & apostolic way of settling disputes than the old & barbarous one, after all these centuries; but when I feel that it must be, few persons are more martial than I, or like better to write of war in prose & rhyme.

But the martial Hardy didn't get into the Boer War poems. We must take his remark in this letter not as description, but as a promise of what was still to come—an epic poem of war that would be both civilized and barbarous.

And then the next war came: The Great War, the War That Would End War, the first Modern War. Hardy's immediate response was complicated because it contained both a private and a public, "official" element. This was a war in which, almost from the first shot, English writers were organized, recruited, drafted into literary battalions for the support of the national effort. The war was not a month old when C. F. G. Masterman, the government official in charge of propaganda, summoned principal English writers to his office in Whitehall "for the organization of public statements of the strength of the British case and principles in the war by well-known men of letters." (This is Hardy's formulation of the project, from his own memorandum.)

Those men of letters included Sir James Barrie, Robert Bridges, Arnold Bennett, Hall Caine, G. K. Chesterton, Arthur Conan Doyle, John Galsworthy, Maurice Hewlett, Anthony

Hope, John Masefield, Henry Newbolt, and H. G. Wells. Too old for the trenches (the youngest, Masefield, was thirty-six), most of them would have supported the war with their pens, officially or not. But Hardy seems different; at seventy-four, he was the oldest of the lot, and he was the most private. Left to himself, he might have written "civilized" poems of private feeling, like those he had written during the Boer War; or he might have fallen silent, as other writers did. But he was summoned by his government, and he went. And having, as it were, enlisted, he returned to Max Gate and promptly wrote an appropriate "public" poem. "Men Who March Away" is dated 5 September 1914—three days after the Whitehall meeting:

> What of the faith and fire within us
>> Men who march away
>> Ere the barn-cocks say
>> Night is growing gray,
> To hazards whence no tears can win us;
> What of the faith and fire within us
>> Men who march away?
>
> Is it a purblind prank, O think you,
>> Friend with the musing eye,
>> Who watch us stepping by
>> With doubt and dolorous sigh?
> Can much pondering so hoodwink you!
> Is it a purblind prank, O think you,
>> Friend with the musing eye?
>
> Nay. We see well what we are doing,
>> Though some may not see—
>> Dalliers as they be!—
>> England's need are we;

Her distress would set us rueing:
Nay. We see well what we are doing,
   Though some may not see!

In our heart of hearts believing
   Victory crowns the just,
   And that braggarts must
   Surely bite the dust,
March we to the field ungrieving,
In our heart of hearts believing
   Victory crowns the just.

Hence the faith and fire within us
   Men who march away
   Ere the barn-cocks say
   Night is growing gray,
To hazards whence no tears can win us;
Hence the faith and fire within us
   Men who march away.[6]

Like the Boer embarkation poems, this is a poem of military departure, marching men observed by a stationary witness. ("You may possibly have suspected," Hardy wrote to his friend Sydney Cockerell, "the 'Friend with the musing eye' to be the author himself.") The situation is one that is common in Hardy: a skeptical poet-watcher, motionless, observing the actions of others. Usually that watcher sees what others do not, but here it is the other way around; the watcher doubts, but the weight of the poem is with the soldiers, who believe in their war.

Hardy was not entirely pleased with the "official" poem he

6. This version was published in the London *Times* (9 September 1914). A different version appears in *Moments of Vision* (1917).

had written. He wrote to his friend Arthur Symons of these lines: "I fear they were not free from some banalities which it is difficult to keep out of lines which are meant to appeal to the man in the street." And indeed it does seem to have been written against his deepest convictions about the war, if you compare it with poems like "Drummer Hodge" and "The Man He Killed."

The general critical response to "Song of the Soldiers" was very favorable—at least among civilian writers, such as the men of letters who gathered at Masterman's meeting; it was good propaganda, the stuff, as we say, to feed the troops. But it was not admired by young soldier-poets: they knew better. Here is a passage from a letter written by Charles Sorley—nineteen years old, not yet a war poet, not yet even in France, but already aware of what was at issue:

> Curiously enough, I think that "Men Who March Away" is the most arid poem in the book [*Satires of Circumstance*], besides being untrue of the sentiments of the ranksman going to war: "Victory crowns the just" is the worst line he ever wrote—filched from a leading article in *The Morning Post*, and unworthy of him who had always previously disdained to insult Justice by offering it a material crown like Victory.[7]

What Sorley expresses in this letter is more than a difference of opinion. He is giving definition to a radical division in English society, between generations, and between civilians and soldiers—a division that will split English culture into two increasingly separate and hostile parts: the men who have fought and know what war is (and are therefore the young) versus those who have not (the Old Men—profiteers and politicians

---

7. Charles Hamilton Sorley, *The Letters of Charles Sorley* (1919), 246.

and generals—and the patriotic women). Out of this sense of division will come the antiwar literature, which is the only literature of that war that we still read, and which has established itself as the continuing Modern Myth of the War. Out of it will also come postwar modernism, and the cultural mood of the 1920s. War poems by Hardy like "Men Who March Away" are not in that modern mode; they seem to place him on the *other* side of the division, with the Old Men and the fierce women. Most of his poems of the First World War fall on that side. No doubt that is why he called them collectively not simply "War Poems," but "Poems of War and Patriotism": *patriotism*, the blustering virtue, is all some of them have—that and German-hating. They do not sound like Hardy, but they are there.

Hardy recognized the contradiction between those public poems and his private feelings. "The difficulty about the war for men at home," he wrote in a letter in 1915, "is that what we feel about it we must not say, & what we must say about it we seldom think." But he accepted the lies that war demanded, and imposed on his sense of the war's reality the romantic falsehoods of wartime convention. He sentimentalized the death of his young nephew Frank George, who was killed at Gallipoli (to call that bloody failure of a campaign a "Game with Death," as he does in "Before Marching and After" is gross sentimentality). And he called down curses on the Germans, whom he represented in the atrocity images of current propaganda. He could not say of these poems, as he said of his Boer War poems, that "not a single one is Jingo or Imperial."

It is tempting to bundle up Hardy's "official" war poems of 1914–18 and discard them all as the works of some other, inferior sensibility—Hardy-in-Whitehall, or the sum of Masterman's committee. It was not that clear, though; Hardy carried into the First World War some of the "martial" spirit that had been in his head since childhood, the spirit he had found in *A History of the Wars* and the stories of the old men. How else are we to explain "Then and Now," written in 1915, in which he repeats with obvious approval the famous daft remark of Lord Charles Hay at the Battle of Fontenoy (1745)? According to legend, Lord Charles, commanding British troops against the French, invited the French guard to fire first. The French replied, "We never fire first: *you* fire first." Here is Hardy's version of that exchange:

> When battles were fought
> With chivalrous sense of Should and Ought,
> In spirit men said,
> "End we quick or dead,
> Honour is some reward!
> Let us fight fair—for our own best or worst;
> So, Gentlemen of the Guard,
> Fire first!

One cannot explain away this foolish poem simply by assigning it to Hardy's false, "official" voice, as though he wasn't responsible for it; he really believed what he said. Here, in support of its argument is a passage from a letter dated August 28, 1914:

> As for myself, the recognition that we are living in a more brutal age than that, say, of Elizabeth, or of the chivalry which could cry: "Gentlemen of the Guard, fire first!" (far more brutal, indeed; no chivalry now!) does not inspire one to write hopeful poetry, or even conjectural prose, but simply make one sit still in apathy, & watch the clock spinning backwards.

There are two Hardy voices in this passage, both audible, both true. One is the martial voice in love with the old wars, the voice that yearns for a war that would be chivalrous and honorable, and so, somehow, "civilized." The other is the dark inward voice, passive and dejected, shocked by the horrors of the war in progress, the voice that describes the war in private letters as "the slaughter in progress," "this ghastly war," "this brutal European massacre," "an accursed thing."

The "Poems of War and Patriotism" are not very good poems—at least as bad as the Boer War poems, but in a different way. Not bad because Hardy did not have much to say, as in 1899–1901, but because what he had to say was trite, banal, "martial," propagandistic, jingoist, embarrassing to an admirer of his greatest lyrics. And because we sense in them his sad admission that "what we feel about it we must not say." The exceptions are few: one wartime poem, one poem forty years old, and one postwar poem—none of them directly concerned with the war itself.

"A New Year's Eve in War Time" is one of Hardy's "literally true" poems: he had stood in his doorway at Max Gate on New Year's Eve, 1915, and had heard a horse gallop by just on the strike of midnight, "as if Death astride came / To numb all with his knock." The poem ends:

> What rider it bears
> There is none to proclaim;
> And the Old Year has struck,
> And, scarce animate,
> The New makes moan.
>
> Maybe that "More Tears!—
> More Famine and Flame—
> More Severance and Shock!"
> Is the order from Fate
> That the Rider speeds on
> To pale Europe; and tiredly the pines intone.

It is another of Hardy's silent, motionless poems: the poet-watcher stands and feels, but says nothing, because there is nothing to be said or done.

The most memorable expression of the private Hardy voice is in his shortest war poem, the exquisite little lyric "In Time of 'The Breaking of Nations.'" The story of its composition is well known—Hardy told it in the *Life and Work*, how he had the experience in the Cornish countryside in 1870, while he was courting his first wife, Emma Gifford; how he watched a farm worker harrowing the arable land while in Europe the Franco-Prussian battle of Gravelotte was being fought; and how he buried that image and its emotion for more than forty years before resurrecting it in the second year of the Great War.

> Only a man harrowing clods
>   In a slow silent walk
> With an old horse that stumbles and nods
>   Half asleep as they stalk.
>
> Only thin smoke without flame
>   From the heaps of couch-grass;
> Yet this will go onward the same
>   Though Dynasties pass.
>
> Yonder a maid and her wight
>   Come whispering by:
> War's annals will cloud into night
>   Ere their story die.

An extraordinary poem—a *pastoral* war poem, so small in scale, so local, yet containing in it the fall of dynasties, the theme that informs Hardy's vast epic drama, and so reminds us of the continuing presence in his imagination of war's claim to greatness—and the universe's denial of that claim. One wants those twelve lines to contain and define the true, essential Hardy-on-war. And so perhaps they do; for they express the theme of endurance and survival and even hope, which runs through *The Dynasts* and which has the last word in the final Chorus of the Pities, and appears in lyrics like "The Darkling Thrush"—the hope that Hardy could not justify philosophically or historically, but could not eradicate from his own heart.

In December 1918, a month after the end of the war, Hardy copied out "Men Who March Away" for his friend Henry Newbolt, and sent it to him with a short note. "My mind goes back," he wrote,

> to the row of poor young fellows in straw hats who had fallen-in in front of our County Hall here—lit by the September sun, whom my rather despondent eye surveyed.
>
> Well, it is all over now—at least I suppose so. I confess that I take a smaller interest in the human race since this outburst than I did before.

And, one might add, a smaller interest in war. The First World War was over, but hope had not triumphed over despair. There had been no epic grandeur in its devastation, no Hector and no Achilles among its troops, nor any Napoleon or Wellington or Nelson. There was no rejoicing in Hardy's message to Newbolt, and none in his heart. He had never expected much of human beings, or of the universe in which they struggled; but the war had lowered his expectations still further. And that, for him, had been its only consequence.

The great poem of this mood, and Hardy's last war poem, is, appropriately, not about the war but about the ending of it. It is titled "And There Was a Great Calm" (as so often, in moments of profound emotion Hardy turned to the Bible for the best phrase), and subtitled "On the Signing of the Armistice, Nov. 11, 1918." It is the one poem in English I know of that records the emotions of that moment with a due sense of their complexity, and the only poem of Hardy's 1914–18 war poems that has entered the canon of First World War verse—one poem among the works of the young soldier-poets by a noncombatant who was old enough to remember the Charge of the Light Brigade.

"And There Was a Great Calm" celebrates nothing. It doesn't say who won or who lost, or why they were fighting, or whether the best side triumphed. It says, rather, what Hardy said privately at the war's beginning, that the war, simply by happening, had destroyed the dream of human progress that Hardy had believed in, in the prewar years, until the "old hopes that earth was bettering slowly / Were dead and damned." Rhetorically, the poem begins in abstractions—Passion, Despair, Anger, Selflessness—and proceeds by emptying itself of them, until it ends in unmodified particulars—the guns silent, the horses not whipped, because the war is ended. Over the vast ruined battlefield, the Spirits from *The Dynasts* hover, denying to this war the epic grandeur that Hardy found in the Napoleonic wars.

Here is the final stanza:

> Calm fell. From Heaven distilled a clemency;
> There was peace on earth, and silence in the sky;
> Some could, some could not, shake off misery:
> The Sinister Spirit sneered: "It had to be!"
> And again the Spirit of Pity whispered, "Why?"

An empty earth and a silent sky, continuing misery for some, and empty fatalism for others, and an unanswered questioning of it all: Hardy had come, at the end, to the point that soldier-poets had also reached—the same bitter vision of war, and of humankind's unalterable capacity for violence against itself.

It is not surprising that those young poets admired him, and traced their poetical descent from him. The evidence is everywhere, in the poems of Sassoon, Graves, and Blunden among the survivors, and of Sorley and Edward Thomas among the dead. He was their ancestor, they were his heirs. (Sassoon and Blunden carried *The Dynasts* with them into the trenches.) What they inherited was partly the starkly formal style, in which one could talk about war without dishonesty and without high rhetoric, and partly the dark vision of existence. But there was another element, too—the Spirit of Pity; Wilfred Owen, you will remember, said of his poems: "The poetry is in the Pity."

The history of Hardy's poetic wars is a history of war in his lifetime—not of actual fighting, but of the evolution of ideas and feelings about war during the nearly three-quarters of a century during which he wrote. In that time, the romance of war receded and its epic grandeur faded. So did the hope that humankind would evolve upward, beyond the use of force against each other. Hardy's poems (including *The Dynasts*) chart those lost imaginings. They also chart a sensitive man's awareness of the sufferings that war inflicted on helpless men and women in his time, and most terribly as war became *modern* war. Hardy never got closer to actual war than the Dorchester street corner from which he watched the young men of Wessex march away; but he felt wars—as a common soldier might feel them, or a general; or a soldier's wife; or a war horse, a coney, an earthworm. And as the presiding Spirits of the universe—the Sinister Spirit, the Ironic Spirit, and the Spirit of the Pities—would feel them, if such spirits existed outside his own head.

War was an important part of the furnishings of Hardy's imagination, as it is of the imaginations of all of us. For war, like love, is a primal subject: we cannot *not* think about it, it is there in our minds because it is in our lives—changing as wars change, and as the hopes and gullibilities of people change, but there. Hardy's wars changed, too, from romantic continental battles commanded by heroes to wars that might be transcended by morally evolving humanity, to the final recognition that war is barbaric and destructive because men are, and always will be.

When Hardy dictated his autobiography to his second wife, Florence, shortly after the First World War, he described the changes that had occurred in the war in his head:

A long study of the European wars of a century earlier had made it appear to him that common-sense had taken the place of bluster in men's minds; and he felt this so strongly that in the very year before war burst on Europe he wrote some verses called "His Country," bearing on the decline of antagonism between peoples; and as long before as 1901 he composed a poem called "The Sick Battle-God," which assumed that zest for slaughter was dying out. It was seldom he had felt so heavy at heart as in seeing his old view of the gradual bettering of human nature, as expressed in these verses of 1901, completely shattered by the events of 1914 and onwards. War, he had supposed, had grown too coldly scientific to kindle again for long all the ardent romance which had characterized it down to Napoleonic times, when the most intense battles were over in a day, and the most exciting tactics and strategy led to the death of comparatively few combatants. Hence nobody was more amazed than he at the German incursion into Belgium, and the contemplation of it led him to despair of the world's history thenceforward.

From romance, to evolutionary meliorism, to pity and despair—you can follow those imaginings in Hardy's writings about war, from the early notes for an epic through to his dark postwar despair in "And There Was a Great Calm." And you can see that there was one stretch of years in that arc, from the end of the last Victorian war to the middle of the first modern one, when a great poet could still write an epic of war because he could hold in his imagination at one time war's grandeur and war's pity. In those years, he wrote his most monumental work and his most perfect small lyric, both war poems, and then was silenced by the reality of the war that came.

*

First published in Thomas Hardy Reappraised,
ed. Keith Wilson (2006).

Yeats's Wars

I begin not with Yeats but with Eric Partridge—not yet the great lexicographer that he became, but a boy of eighteen, on a training-camp march in the winter of 1914–15.

> The early-winter morning was fresh and cold, yet not sharp; the air, without bite, had an invigorating tang; the sun shone clear, though weak, through the trees, merely to be alive was a joy, young legs moving freely, easily, young eyes seeing every frosted leaf aglisten, young voices singing some foolish song, young hearts astir with their entry into war, war which, next to love, has most captured the world's imagination. ("Frank Honywood, Private")

I quote this for the sake of that closing phrase: *war which, next to love.* . . . That is my subject, and especially the point that Partridge makes about it, its power over the world's imagination. What concerns me is not war-as-history, not the battles and the generals, but war as a constituent part of human imaginations, and particularly of one great imagination, that of W. B. Yeats.

You will note, in Partridge's recollection, that he is not talking about the experience of war; at that point in his life he had not had any. Yet war had the power to stir him even then; it existed in his mind as an *idea*—a motive for the march that would take him eventually to witness death and suffering at Gallipoli and on the Western Front. And perhaps you will notice another curious thing in the Partridge quotation: the association of war not with death, but with energy and life.

Where do such ideas of war come from to inhabit the minds of children? (And of us all: for we all partake of the world's imagination—war has captured us, too.) I can make a fair guess about one kind of source, in the case of Partridge. He was a first-year classics student at the University of Queensland, in Australia, when the Great War began. He would have known his Homer and Virgil and Horace. Shakespeare, too, no doubt, and some Victorian poets—Tennyson, Kipling. And on his own he'd have read Henty and his imitators, all those adventure stories of boys in battle, with titles like *With Roberts to Pretoria* and *With Kitchener in the Soudan*, that set up the volunteers of 1914 for their sad destinies. When we are young, our understandings of abstractions like Love and War come mainly from imagined versions, from literature and art: where else could they come from?

In the case of war they might also come from history; for war is there in the world and always has been. I think it was Will Durant who calculated that there have been only twenty-nine years in all of human history during which there was not a war in progress, somewhere. And surely if he had looked harder he could have filled in those empty years; for the history of mankind, as Colonel Repington remarked in *The First World War*, is the history of war.

When Partridge wrote "war which, next to love," he wasn't thinking about history or the classics—he was thinking of the symbolic forces that move and perhaps explain our lives, the primal myths of the world's imagination. In our imaginations, *war* is the name we give to the extremes of violence in our lives, the dark dividing opposite of the connecting myth, which we call *love*. War enacts the great antagonisms of history, the agones of nations; but it also offers metaphors for those other antagonisms, the private battles of our private lives, our conflicts with one another and with the world, and with ourselves. We are all soldiers in the war between men and women, for example; and when Isabella in *Measure for Measure* says "I am at war 'twixt will and will not," it isn't only the military men in the audience who know what she means.

The imagination's wars are more than conflict: they are also the occasions of imagined action, of heroism and personal victory. Words like *warrior* and *battle* and *defeat* range outward in our vocabularies, from the context of actual combat into all those human situations in which energy meets opposition, in which somebody wins and somebody loses. We have not all been soldiers, but we have all had our wars. And we have found images in art and literature to express our feelings about those wars.

And so it was with Yeats, a poet who never wore a uniform or fired a shot or witnessed any battle, but whose imagination and art were nevertheless full of wars and armies, soldiers and swords and blood. We have a careful and detailed account of the furnishing of that imagination in Yeats's *Reveries over Childhood and Youth*—that's what the book is, a kind of inventory of the resonant particulars that furnished his young mind. Many of those particulars are military: Yeats notes, for example, that in the house of his Pollexfen grandfather there were colored prints of Crimean War battles, and that one of the Pollexfen ships had been a blockade-runner in the American Civil War, and on the other side of his family, among the Yeats ancestors, he mentions one of Marlborough's generals. So there were battles and soldiers and daring deeds around him in his earliest childhood, feeding his imagination.

Two passages from Yeats's account of his early years are especially arresting. Here, first, is Yeats's description of his friendship with a stable boy:

> He had a book of Orange rhymes, and the days when we read them together in the hayloft gave me the pleasure of rhyme for the first time. Later on I can remember being told, when there was a rumour of a Fenian rising, that rifles had been served out to the Orangemen; and presently, when I had begun to dream of my future life, I thought I would like to die fighting the Fenians. I was to build a very fast and beautiful ship and to have under my command a company of young men who were always to be in training like athletes and so become as brave and handsome as the young men in the storybooks, and there was to be a big battle on the sea-shore near Rosses and I was to be killed.

The early identification with the Orangemen anticipates, perhaps, Yeats's later ambivalent feelings about conflicting forces in Ireland, but it is not really surprising—many young lives begin with such unexamined political loyalties (I was a Republican until I was twelve—not an Irish one, an American one). What is more significant is the association of fighting with poetry, and of beauty with the dream of a fighting ship, and the romantic fantasy of death in battle. Fighting is beautiful, and the stuff of poetry; and death is romantic.

A second passage also involves the sharing of literature with other boys—in this case schoolmates in London.

> I read their boys' books and they excited me, but if I read of some English victory, I did not believe that I read of my own people. They thought of Cressy and Agincourt and the Union Jack and were all very patriotic, and I, without those memories of Limerick and the Yellow Ford that would have

strengthened an Irish Catholic, thought of mountain and lake, of my grandfather and of ships. Anti-Irish feeling was running high, for the Land League had been founded and landlords had been shot, and I, who had no politics, was yet full of pride, for it is romantic to live in a dangerous country.

What this adds to the inventory of components, in addition to the evidence of boys' adventure-stories read, is the curious situation of an imaginative boy, excited by tales of battle, but without a cause, thrilled by the idea of danger, but deprived of an imagined motive for it. The name for this whole set of attitudes in literature is *Romance*, and in some circumstances *Epic* (I note that Yeats also read a prose version of the *Iliad* at about this time—and we know how powerful the figures and images of that poem were for his own poetry throughout his life).

To these constituents of Yeats's young imagination we must add two others from the years of his early manhood. First, a visit from Maud Gonne, when Yeats was in his early twenties:

Presently a hansom drove up to our door at Bedford Park with Miss Maud Gonne, who brought an introduction to my father from old John O'Leary, the Fenian leader. She vexed my father by praise of war, war for its own sake, not as the creator of certain virtues but as if there were some virtue in excitement itself. I supported her against my father, which vexed him more, though he might have understood that . . . a man young as I could not have differed from a woman so beautiful and so young.

War for its own sake, excitement as a *virtue*: that became a possible idea, a part of Yeats's myth of war, because of Maud Gonne.

The other influence on Yeats's imagination at this time was that strange man MacGregor Mathers, whose studies, Yeats said, "were two only—magic and the theory of war." "He began to foresee changes in the world," Yeats wrote in *The Trembling of the Veil*:

> announcing in 1893 or 1894 the imminence of immense wars, and was it in 1895 or 1896 that he learned ambulance work, and made others learn it? He had a sabre wound on his wrist—or perhaps his forehead, for my memory is not clear—got in some student riot that he had mistaken for the beginning of war. It may have been some talk of his that made me write the poem that begins:—
>
> The dews drop slowly and dreams gather: unknown spears
> Suddenly hurtle before my dream-awakened eyes,
> And then the clash of fallen horsemen and the cries
> Of unknown perishing armies beat about my ears.
>
> Was this prophecy of his, which would shortly be re-peated by mediums and clairvoyants all over the world, an unconscious inference taken up into an imagination brood-ing upon war, or was it prevision?

Like Maud Gonne, Mathers seems to have thought about war not as events occurring in history, but simply as action, as the violent instrument of change. His imagination, "brooding upon war," penetrated Yeats's imagination—and Yeats's poetry, too, as the quoted lines demonstrate.

These, then, are the factors that shaped the young Willie Yeats's idea of war, during the years from early childhood to the time when his first books of verse began to appear. Starting from the beginning: family history, literature (Orange rhymes, boys' books, the *Iliad*), a beautiful revolutionary, a mad magi-cian. The wars that they offered were romantic and imaginary, heroic, immense, and virtuous in themselves. There is no actual current war in this list, nor even any historical one historically considered (the Crimean War enters Yeats's mind only as *pictures*). Nor is there any sense of political commitment, of any right cause worth dying for; the thing worth dying for, in this romantic vision, is dying itself.

One can't say that this is an *Irish* imagination being formed, except in the negative sense of being excluded from English loyalties. It is, instead, an epic and romantic imagination, the kind that values the excitement of conflict more than victory, and that in fact honors and romanticizes the loser—so long as he dies fighting (as we all do with Hector and Roland). It is not an imagination caught up in history, as Hardy's was caught in the Napoleonic wars; it will not construct its myths of war out of actual events, as Hardy did in *The Dynasts*. Instead it will be the opposite kind of imagination—an idealizing, symbolizing one.

If we turn to the early poems, we will find there the wars and battles that this kind of imagination creates: mythological, heroic, symbolical wars. They are fought by heroes, outside of history, and are not events so much as cycles, recurrences, continuities of conflict. The pattern is set in the earliest example, *The Wanderings of Oisin*, in which the Hero, transported over the sea by his faery-bride Niamh, spends a century on each of three islands. The first is the Island of Dancing, and the third is the Island of Forgetfulness—two modes of escape from the sadness of mortality. The second island has two names, the Isle of Many Fears and the Island of Victories, and clearly these two identifying qualities go together: what the Hero fights is not this enemy or that, but Fear itself. That's what Heroism *is*— and like Dancing and Forgetfulness, it is a mode of escape from human sorrow.

On this second island, Oisin confronts a protean, unsubduable demon, whom he fights again and again. In every fight the demon is defeated: and each time he returns, healed anew, to fight again. And so Oisin

> for a hundred years
> So warred, so feasted, with nor dreams nor fears,
> Nor languor nor fatigue: an endless feast,
> An endless war.

Oisin is Yeats's first warrior-hero. He is the man of perfect energy, who expresses that energy in loving, feasting, and fighting (later Yeats would add the creation of Art as another expression of the same force). The war that he fights is no particular war, and he fights it against no particular enemy (the demon of the Isle of Many Fears, like the dragon of medieval romance, simply represents the opposing Other, the Hero's antagonist). This war has no direction and no end: it continues, in endlessly recurring cycles, until the poem ends. The Hero cannot be defeated in this war, but he will not win, either, not in the end: time and mortality will vanquish him at last. His heroism lies in the fact that he knows this, and fights in spite of it—or because of it. "I hear my soul drop down into decay," Oisin grown old tells his tormenter, Saint Patrick,

> And Manannan's dark tower, stone after stone,
> Gather sea-slime and fall the seaward way,
> And the moon goad the waters night and day,
> That all be overthrown.

> But till the moon has taken all, I wage
> War on the mightiest men under the skies,
> And they have fallen or fled, age after age.

Many motifs here will echo throughout Yeats's poems: the tower and the moon, the heroism and the ultimate, inevitable overthrow—a Yeatsian story is being told that will be told again and again, from "Cuchulain's Fight with the Sea" to "The Black Tower."

The poem that Yeats quoted in *The Trembling of the Veil*, as an example of Mathers's influence, is "The Valley of the Black Pig."

> The dews drop slowly and dreams gather: unknown spears
> Suddenly hurtle before my dream-awakened eyes,
> And then the clash of fallen horsemen and the cries
> Of unknown perishing armies beat about my ears.
> We who still labour by the cromlech on the shore,
> The grey cairn on the hill, when the day sinks drowned
>   in dew,
> Being weary of the world's empires, bow down to you,
> Master of the still stars and of the flaming door.

It is an inscrutable poem—even Yeats thought that it needed glossing. In its first appearance in *The Wind Among the Reeds* he attached a note to it that runs nearly two pages, and he is mostly concerned with explaining the "war" that the poem images.

One clue to the poem's meaning is its original title: it was first published as one of "Two Poems concerning Peasant Visionaries." So it is a visionary poem, about a visionary war. Yeats explained this point further in his note:

> All over Ireland there are prophecies of the coming rout of the enemies of Ireland, in a certain Valley of the Black Pig, and these prophecies are, no doubt, now, as they were in the Fenian days, a political force. I have heard of one man who

would not give any money to the Land League, because the Battle could not be until the close of the century; but, as a rule, periods of trouble bring prophecies of its near coming. A few years before my time, an old man who lived at Lisadell, in Sligo, used to fall down in a fit and rave out descriptions of the Battle; and a man in Sligo has told me that it will be so great a battle that the horses shall go up to their fetlocks in blood, and that their girths, when it is over, will rot from their bellies for lack of a hand to unbuckle them.

This is not Maud Gonne's war, but Mathers's: a vision of an ultimate apocalyptic battle, a great change. But Yeats's note makes it more than that. "The battle," he says, "is a mythological one," and he offers a source in Irish mythology, and analogies in *The Golden Bough*, and in local superstition, before he concludes:

> The Battle should, I believe, be compared with three other battles; a battle the Sidhe are said to fight when a person is being taken away by them; a battle they are said to fight in November for the harvest; the great battle the Tribes of the goddess Danu fought, according to the Gaelic chroniclers, with the Fomor at Moy Tura, or the Towery Plain. . . .
>   I suggest that the battle between the Tribes of the goddess Danu, the powers of light, and warmth, and fruitfulness, and goodness, and the Fomor, the powers of darkness, and cold, and barrenness, and badness upon the Towery Plain, was the establishment of the habitable world, the rout of the ancestral darkness; that the battle among the Sidhe for the harvest is the annual battle of summer and winter; that the battle among the Sidhe at a man's death is the battle of life and death; and that the battle of the Black Pig is the battle between the manifest world and the ancestral darkness at

the end of all things; and that all these battles are one, the battle of all things with shadowy decay. Once a symbolism has possessed the imagination of large numbers of men, it becomes, as I believe, an embodiment of disembodied powers, and repeats itself in dreams and visions, age after age.

This does not explicate the poem; instead it summarizes possible meanings of war as a symbol. The meanings that Yeats offers are the cyclical struggles of mortal life: light against darkness, summer against winter, life against death. These are the struggles that men cannot win, but that they must nevertheless fight (you will notice in the poem that the horsemen are fallen and the unknown armies perishing). They constitute the vision of the heroic life as energy-in-defeat that will remain in Yeats's poetry all of his life. Already in this early poem Yeats is building his system, and building it on *war*.

But not on historical war, either past or present. None of the martial particulars of his childhood—the Crimean battles, the Marlborough general, the blockade-running ship—get into his poems. Neither does the Boer war, though it was fought for nearly three years at the century's end—the years from *The Wind Among the Reeds* to *The Celtic Twilight*. The war was in his mind, all right: he wrote pro-Boer letters to the press, and supported Maud Gonne in her antirecruiting campaign. But he didn't make poems out of it, as for example Hardy did; poetical war remained a symbolic act.

Why this was so is clear enough: the Boer war was an English imperialistic war, and like the wars in the boys' adventure books that Yeats read as a child, it had nothing to do with him. That Yeats was also indifferent to the First World War is more surprising, for that was a war that possessed imaginations— Irish imaginations as well as English ones, to judge from the recruiting figures, and from the flood of war poetry, too.

Not that Yeats wasn't aware of the war. He mentions it often in his letters—passing bits of strategic gossip, the way any civilian would. But for him it was mainly a practical problem, especially in its effects on the Abbey Theatre ("the anxiety of the war and the many deaths reduced our audiences both in Dublin . . . and in England till we are losing heavily"), and on his sister's needlework ("owing to the war it is hard to get good colours"). When Henry James asked Yeats for a contribution to a charitable book, *The Book of the Homeless*, Yeats responded with a poem entitled "A Reason for Keeping Silent" (later he retitled it "On Being Asked for a War Poem").

> I think it better that at times like these
> We poets keep our mouths shut, for in truth
> We have no gift to set a statesman right;
> He's had enough of meddling who can please
> A young girl in the indolence of her youth
> Or an old man upon a winter's night.

One can't help remarking that this reluctance to meddle is entirely out of character: Yeats had been meddling in verse for the past decade—in politics, in theater affairs, and in the Hugh Lane controversy—and he would meddle again. But not in this war; it wasn't *his* war.

That sense of detachment from the war is the subject of Yeats's one memorable poem about the First World War, "An Irish Airman Foresees His Death." The speaker is ostensibly Major Robert Gregory, but he surely speaks for the poet when he says:

> Those that I fight I do not hate,
> Those that I guard I do not love;
> My country is Kiltartan Cross,

My countrymen Kiltartan's poor,
No likely end could bring them loss
Or leave them happier than before.
Nor law, nor duty bade me fight,
Nor public men, nor cheering crowds.

These lines partly present Yeats's idea of the Hero, made solitary by his greatness. But Yeats's Irishness also speaks here, making Kiltartan Cross a country, localizing loyalty to the space of a crossroads. (Remember how, in his childhood fantasies of heroism, he fought his great battle on the seashore near Rosses.) An English war fought in France was too remote, too linked to a history that was not Ireland's, to engage an Irish imagination.

But there was a war that *was* Irish, and that war Yeats could both feel and imagine: the Irish Troubles, the whole run of events from the Easter Uprising to the end of the civil war. "Our war," he called it, and certainly it was his—it was fought all around him, by persons he knew. From his tower, Thoor Ballylee, he could see the flames of burning houses, and his house in Dublin had bullet holes in its windows. With this war the theme of war in Yeats's poetry departs from epic and romance, and enters history.

We can fix the precise day on which that change occurred: April 24, 1916—the day of the Uprising. The poem that Yeats wrote about that day takes the historical date as its title—"Easter 1916": it is one of only a handful of Yeats poems that so announce their historical location. What the poem says is that when war becomes actual, when it is fought not by heroes but by men and women one knows, in places one has seen, reality is changed, and the imagination changes too. The Troubles brought history into Yeats's imagination, but they brought something else—a sense of the reality of evil that I do not find in his earlier work.

In 1922, during the civil war, Yeats wrote to Olivia Shakespear from Thoor Ballylee:

> All we can see from our windows is beautiful and quiet and has been so; yet two miles off near Coole, which is close to the main-road, the Black and Tans flogged young men and then tied them to their lorries by the heels and dragged them along the road till their bodies were torn to pieces. I wonder will literature be much changed by that most momentous of events, the return of evil.

In the case of Yeats's poetry the answer is surely yes.

Out of the intersection of history and evil comes tragedy—not only in the sense of catastrophic public events, but also in the personal sense of a role to be played, an ideal of behavior in an evil time. The word *tragedy* comes late into Yeats's poetic vocabulary, does not in fact appear until "The Tower," then again in "Among School Children" and "Ribh at the Tomb of Baile and Aillinn," and at the end in "Lapis Lazuli"; the adjective *tragic*, except for one early use, begins with "Ego Dominus Tuus," written in 1917, and recurs in poems of the 1930s. The concept itself enters with "Easter 1916," when "a terrible beauty is born."

For Yeats the Irish Troubles made history tragic, and so released a major theme into his poetry. "We begin to live when we have conceived life as tragedy," he wrote in 1921, at the height of the civil war; and for the rest of his life he did see life—and imagine life—in that way. And the history of those years confirmed his vision; for if any time in modern history merits the term *tragic*, it is the last two decades of Yeats's life, the years *entre deux guerres*.

The first great war-poems of Yeats's tragic vision are his two odes, "Nineteen Hundred and Nineteen" and "Meditations in Time of Civil War"; and from them we can see how much the war in Yeats's imagination was changed by events. Both poems are dated in the published text—1919 and 1923, respectively—and one carries its location in history in its title, as "Easter 1916" did. The war that they treat of is clearly and insistently a historical one; it is the war in Ireland that Yeats saw, or heard of, day by day. Both poems contain details of that war—an affable irregular, a Black-and-Tan officer, a dead young soldier, a mother murdered at her door—and by these details Yeats establishes it as a personal war, his war.

Yet the poems are not about war in a narrative sense: there are no battles. Nor in an epic or romantic sense, either: there are no heroes, no victories, no brave deaths. You might say that actual war provided Yeats with the occasion; but that what was going on in his imagination was something larger. Perhaps the best description of what that was is in a line from "Meditations"— "Befitting emblems of adversity." What these poems offer is a new symbolism of war—symbolic still, but including history, and tragedy. Both poems are broken into discontinuous parts, some particular and some fantastic, each a complex symbol. But not of war, exactly; rather of the adversities that war—*this* war—imposed on its victims, and on the imagination: the loss of belief in order and tradition, the destruction of many ingenious lovely things, the return of evil, the death of civilization. And, running through both poems, the hard questions: what can a poet do, what can Art do, in such a tragic time? Answers to those questions preoccupied Yeats for the rest of his life: "late Yeats" begins here, and tragedy released by history gives that final period its unity—an idea of tragedy that grew more energetic, more violent, and more joyous as the times grew darker.

Yeats's last years are for most of us the years of his greatest achievements. But they are also troubling years, in which the greatness and the violence conflict, and Yeats says things that one wishes he hadn't said, or even thought. The most troubling of those utterances focuses on war, and what it came to mean to him in the last decade of his life. In the thirties, the war in his imagination became aggressively positive, as though Yeats was determined to reaffirm Maud Gonne's vision of war-as-virtue, and his own sense of war as an expression of energy (and therefore a creative force), against the vision of war that history had forced upon him—war as the return of evil, war as human adversity.

You will see what I mean if you consider two paragraphs from *Stories of Michael Robartes and His Friends*, first published in 1931, and later incorporated in the second *Vision*. They are ostensibly the recorded remarks of Robartes, Yeats's magus-figure and alter ego:

> After an age of necessity, truth, goodness, mechanism, science, democracy, abstraction, peace, comes an age of freedom, fiction, evil, kindred, art, aristocracy, particularity, war. Has our age burned to the socket?
>
> Dear predatory birds, prepare for war, prepare your children and all that you can reach, for how can a nation or a kindred without war become "that bright particular star" of Shakespeare, that lit the roads in boyhood? Test art, morality, custom, thought, by Thermopylae; make rich and poor act so to one another that they can stand together there. "Love war because of its horror, that belief may be changed, civilisation renewed. We desire belief and lack it. Belief comes from shock and is not desired. When a kindred discovers through apparition and horror that the perfect cannot perish nor even the imperfect long be interrupted, who can withstand that kindred? Belief is renewed continually in the ordeal of death."

First, war as one term in the antinomy of war and peace—necessary, inevitable, eternally cyclical, and therefore morally neutral. And second, war as energy, the instrument of change—and therefore creative, even heroic. These are texts emptied of actual history: the murdered mother and the dead boy, whose stories make the odes human, have been cast aside, that the energetic force of war may be celebrated, even in a tragic world. Yeats has abandoned what his own Irish history had forced upon him, in order to keep the symbolism of war.

You can see how central that symbolism was to Yeats's later thinking in a little poem written in August 1934, "The Four Ages of Man," one of the "Supernatural Songs":

> He with body waged a fight,
> But body won; it walks upright.
>
> Then he struggled with the heart;
> Innocence and peace depart.
>
> Then he struggled with the mind;
> His proud heart he left behind.
>
> Now his wars on God begin;
> At stroke of midnight God shall win.

Four ages as four battles, all lost, the last against God. Human life as wars lost—but always metaphorical wars. Yeats had cast out the real ones from his imagination.

Understanding this radical rejection, we can deal with another problematical text, Yeats's introduction to *The Oxford Book of Modern Verse* (1936), and his decision to exclude the major poets of the First World War from his anthology.

I have a distaste for certain poems written in the midst of the great war. . . . The writers of these poems were invariably officers of exceptional courage and capacity, one a man constantly selected for dangerous work, all, I think, had the Military Cross; their letters are vivid and humorous, they were not without joy—for all skill is joyful—but felt bound, in the words of the best known, to plead the suffering of their men. In poems that had for a time considerable fame, written in the first person, they made that suffering their own. I have rejected these poems for the same reason that made Arnold withdraw his *Empedocles on Etna* from circulation; passive suffering is not a theme for poetry.

Yeats seemed genuinely to have despised Wilfred Owen in particular—"all blood, dirt, and sucked sugar-stick" he called him in a letter to Dorothy Wellesley—but his reasons for not including Owen's poems are more than literary, and have to do with the form that war had taken in Yeats's imagination, here in the mid-thirties. Historical war is once more absent: how the Great War was fought, and for what cause, and by whom—these questions do not figure in Yeats's judgment. Instead he dwells on the courage, skill, and *joy*—an essential term in Yeats's vocabulary of tragedy—of the officer-poets, making them thus *heroic*, and potentially the authors of heroic poems. But instead of writing those poems, they chose, Yeats says, "to plead the suffering of their men." Of their *men*, you will notice—as though suffering were an ailment of the lower classes, like rickets. And they *chose*: Yeats would make their deviation from heroism a voluntary act, as he would make all the human responses to the world that matter willful.

In the *Oxford Book* introduction, Yeats wrote about the First World War as though it had no history, because he could not *imagine* it—could not, that is, adjust his imagination to the historical reality. He could see the Easter Uprising as tragic, because he knew it: it was local and Irish, and was fought by Irishmen who chose to fight, against impossible odds—and so to lose.

That is, it was historical, but it was also heroic—in his version, Cuchulain stalked through the Post Office, epic and romance were possible. But the Western Front was something else: a vast, virtually stationary war fought by anonymous millions, a will-less, suffering, unheroic war, beyond epic, beyond romance, beyond symbolism even. War *couldn't* mean *that*; if it did, its value as an emblem of extreme energy would be lost. So Yeats threw out the poets who had said that that was what it *did* mean, denying the validity of their vision by a willful act of his own.

There is one last expression of the war in Yeats's imagination, and it stands, appropriately, last among the lyric poems in the *Collected Poems* (1950): it is the third part of "Under Ben Bulben." Here Yeats, aware of the approach of death, addresses his posterity, the Irish artists who will come after him.

> You that Mitchel's prayer have heard,
> "Send war in our time, O Lord!"
> Know that when all words are said
> And a man is fighting mad,
> Something drops from eyes long blind,
> He completes his partial mind,
> For an instant stands at ease,
> Laughs aloud, his heart at peace.
> Even the wisest man grows tense
> With some sort of violence
> Before he can accomplish fate,
> Know his work or choose his mate.

The poem is dated September 4, 1938. A historian would note that that was in the middle of the Czechoslovakian crisis: Chamberlain would fly to Munich in a few days to give in to Hitler; trenches were being dug in London parks; gas masks were being distributed. The imminence of the Second World

War was obvious to everyone in Europe. But for Yeats that was merely history, and had nothing to do with the posthumous poem that he was writing; so he could quote Mitchel's "'Send war in our time, O Lord!'" without irony. To him that prayer meant: send *symbolic* war, send violent energy, send antinomial conflict, send heroism and individual will and creativity, make the world *change*!

There is something splendid in the fervor of the old poet, near death, proclaiming his young man's values, still excited by war. But there is also something less admirable, something willful and excluding in his refusal to live in the actual history of his time—a time when the return of evil should have been apparent and unavoidable, when the Lord *was* sending war in our time.

For Yeats, that refusal seems to have been a necessary condition of writing poetry at all in those tragic years, and we can scarcely regret the decision that made "Lapis Lazuli" and "Under Ben Bulben" possible. But we can see its cost. In order to see life as tragedy Yeats had to see war as necessary, and to celebrate the heroic human will that chose to create in spite of war's destruction. But that defiant gesture had been overtaken by history: war had changed in his lifetime—it had lost those properties that made romance and heroism possible. Reality, you might say, changed forever on the Somme. Yeats's response to that change must seem to us imperfect; no argument that I can offer will make "Love war because of its horror" a tolerable statement. But perhaps we can understand it, and the dynamics of the interaction of art and history in his creative life that made such a statement possible. That, essentially, is what this essay has been about—the war in Yeats's imagination.

War and *imagination* take us back to the beginning, to Partridge's words: "war which, next to love, has most captured the world's imagination." What that clause says is that war is a property of the imagination like love—as powerful, and shaped by comparable forces from inside and outside the imagining self. About Love and the world's imagination we have many books, studies like Denis de Rougemont's *Love in the Western World*, but where is our *War in the Western World*? Who has examined the ways in which humankind's habitual and continuous acts of violence against itself have furnished the minds and works of the world's artists, and how those works in turn have shaped the ways in which *we* think and feel about war? Here is a subject in which art and reality interact in subtle and profound ways, in an interaction that has a history as old as the history of love, and with perhaps as many great examples. What I am urging is that critics give some serious attention to war as a shaping presence in art, as it is in the human story. Let us revise Michael Robartes's startling remark: not "Love war because of its horror," but "Study war because of its power"—over our lives, over our minds, over our art. Because it is there, like Love, in the world's imagination.

*

First published in the Sewanee Review *(Winter 1989).*

Ignorantly into War

VERA BRITTAIN

Chronicle of Youth is a selection from Vera Brittain's diary for the years 1913 to 1917. It recounts her pre-war life in Buxton, her first year at the University of Oxford, her wartime experiences as a nurse, and the death of her fiancé. All of these events will be familiar to anyone who has read *Testament of Youth*, or has seen the televised version of the book, and one may well ask if it is really necessary to publish the diary separately, especially since *Testament of Youth* quotes from it so copiously. During Brittain's lifetime, the answer was a firm *No*. She twice tried to find a publisher for selections, but without success. Some reviewers of *Testament* have come to the same conclusion—that enough Vera Brittain is enough.

But I think they are wrong.

The two books are, in fact, very different. The difference is not simply that between raw material and finished product. It might be better described as a difference in mode of narrative. The diary is a young girl's version of her life as a romance, with herself as the romantic heroine (modeled very obviously on Lyndall, in Olive Schreiner's *The Story of an African Farm*, a book that was a kind of sacred text for both Brittain and her soldier-fiancé, Roland Leighton). It is full of high emotions, and bits of verse, and girlish philosophizing, all put down straight and without irony, as Lyndall herself might have written them. *Testament of Youth*, on the other hand, is history—retrospective, interpretive, and judgmental, and, since it is autobiographical history, much concerned to explain and justify, and above all to separate the woman who wrote in 1933 from that earlier self who did the living and the emoting, and was so young and ignorant.

Here is one small example of the difference. In *Testament*, Brittain's brother Edward wants to join the army at once in August 1914, but their father forbids it: "having himself escaped immersion in the public-school tradition, which stood for militaristic heroism unimpaired by the damping exercise of reason, he withheld his permission for any kind of military training." Irony, distance, and pacifism are all at work here. The diary reports the episode in this way: "Daddy was quite angry about the letter being sent to the War Office, but E. said that Daddy, not being a public-school man or having had any training could not possibly understand the impossibility of his remaining in inglorious safety while others, scarcely older than he, were offering their all." Poor Edward, one thinks, believing such rubbish; poor Daddy, despised by his priggish son; poor Vera, not seeing what she would say twenty years later.

The Vera Brittain of the diary appears first in 1913, as a quite ordinary pre-war provincial eighteen-year-old, fond of dancing, clothes, bridge, and flirtation, but also serious, vain about her own intelligence (which is not in fact all that evident), and rather patronizing toward her family and her town. She is above all ignorant of everything that might have helped her to live through the years to come. "On the way to golf," she writes on March 4, 1913, "I induced Mother to disclose a few points on sexual matters which I thought I ought to know, though the information is always intensely distasteful to me & most depressing—in fact it quite put me off my game!" And sex is not the only area of knowledge in which she is deficient: she seems to have no notion that she might educate herself further at a university, or that she might have a professional career (she writes instead of "literary aspirations"); and she never notices the public world of politics until, on July 25, 1914, she mentions "the European crisis" in a paragraph that begins: "In spite of the showeryness of the day, we managed to have our match against Fallowfield."

It is this ordinary, rather dreary girl who blunders ignorantly into life in the diary of the war years. When war is declared, her first reaction is excitement: "That which has been so long anticipated by some & scoffed at by others has come to pass at last—Armageddon in Europe!" And at once her comments on the causes and progress of the war are stuffed with the rhetoric and the clichés of the popular press: "mailed fists" and "tottering hopes for peace" and "terrible retribution." To this non-information, she adds rumors: the Serbs have invaded Austria, Francis Joseph is dead. Reading these pages one realizes, sadly, that Brittain and her generation had no chance of coming closer to the truth than that, and that many of them made their decisions and lost their lives without knowing *anything* about the realities of the war they were in.

Burdened as she was by propaganda and rumor, it is perhaps not so surprising that Brittain learned the lessons of war very slowly. In September 1915, she approved when British soldiers smashed the shop of a German hairdresser in Buxton: they were enemy aliens, she thought, and ought to have been interned long ago. And she stuck to the rhetoric of leader-writers and Rupert Brooke, even when young men she loved were in the trenches: life, she writes, is bare "of all but the few great things which are all we have to cling to now—honour & love and heroism & sacrifice." Her fiancé, Roland Leighton, knew better than that, and wrote against rhetoric from the trenches:

Let him who thinks that War is a glorious golden thing, who
loves to roll forth stirring words of exhortation, invoking
Honour and Praise and Valour and Love of country . . . let
him look at a little pile of sodden grey rags that cover half a
skull and a shin bone and what might have been Its ribs, or
at this skeleton lying on its side . . . and let him realise how
grand & glorious a thing it is to have distilled all Youth and
Joy and Life into a foetid heap of hideous putrescence. Who
is there who has known and seen who can say that Victory is
worth the deaths of even one of these?

Vera Brittain quotes this letter in *Testament*, and adds: "Had
there really been a time, I wondered, when I believed that it
was?" The diary shows that, indeed, there *had* been a time, and
that it had lasted surprisingly long—she is still quoting Rupert
Brooke on the last page, the poem about leaving a white un-
broken glory. She had learned some things, but she was still in
her way ignorant, ordinary, and of her time. The wisdom, such
as it was, came later.

But that doesn't matter, for what is valuable in the diary has
almost nothing to do with Brittain's individual merit, or her development as a thinking person, but rather with her represen-
tativeness, as a young girl living through the moral confusion
and the suffering of the First World War, one day at a time.
Along the way, she offers interesting materials for a social history of her world: pre-war middle-class Buxton; Somerville in
1914; nursing in Camberwell; and the customs of a war-time
courtship (one kiss *after* she and Leighton had agreed to be
engaged). But at the center is the endless daily wretchedness
of a young woman in love with a man who might die tomorrow, who might even have died yesterday, for a cause that she
confusedly still believed in and that he didn't (and who did die

pointlessly and without glory, mending barbed wire on a moon-
lit night at the end of 1915).

Vera Brittain thought that 1939, "with its intense, life-
and-death preoccupation with war and peace," might be an
appropriate time to publish her diary. Today, that preoccupation seems no less intense, and so the time must be equally
appropriate—though one can't help adding gloomily that if
literature were really an effective instrument against war the
world would be at peace by now.

*

First published in the Times Literary Supplement,
October 30, 1981.

Rebecca West's
The Return of the Soldier

When Rebecca West wrote *The Return of the Soldier*, she was living a secluded life in a house in the country outside London, with only her three-year-old son and a woman servant for company. Why she was there, twenty-four years old, without a husband and apart from society, is not really our business (her biographers will tell you all about that, if you want to know); but the fact of her seclusion *is* our business, because it affected the book she wrote. For *The Return of the Soldier* is a novel of extraordinary isolation. In an English country house four people touch and disturb each other's lives in the course of four days: that's all the story. There is no encompassing society, no action that reaches out from the house into the larger world, no great flow of passing time. Jane Austen wrote that the scale of her novels was "the little bit (two inches wide) of ivory on which I work with so fine a brush"; but she was lavish in her casts of characters and her expanse of space and time, compared with the claustrophobic narrowness out of which Rebecca West made her novel. It is an extraordinary book, a perfect small work of art, no longer than a Conrad tale or a James *nouvelle*, that makes its perfection out of its limitations: a novel of the enclosed world of a few entangled private lives.

Yet for all its private constriction, *The Return of the Soldier* also belongs in the public world, in the great shared story that we call history. It was written during 1916 and 1917, and its action is located precisely in that period: in March 1916. Those dates matter: they set both the writing of the novel and the actions it describes at the dark dead center of the First World War. In the spring of 1916, the war had settled into a bloody stalemate along the trenches of the Western Front. Battles were fought, and men died, and there were more battles, and more deaths; but there were no victories, and no great advances, only casualties that mounted into millions. No one knew how or when the war would end, or how many lives it would cost before the last shot was fired; in 1916 there was only the dying.

The Western Front was a long way from the Thames valley where the novel is set, but it is a haunting presence there (as it was everywhere in England during those years), and an important element in the story. The title tells us that the man in the story is a soldier returned from the war (though by the time we've reached the end *return* will have another, darker meaning). And so, for all the strict enclosure of the novel's private world, the public world presses in, and makes *The Return* a novel of another kind—a war novel.

It is, to be sure, an unusual sort of war novel, without battles or battlefields, and with only one soldier, and told by a woman who has never seen this or any other war, who indeed seems to have known nothing at all of the world beyond Baldry Court. Yet the war exists for her: she can visualize No Man's Land, the barbed wire and the shells and the muddy trenches, and the dismembered bodies, and the rotting faces of the dead.

Jenny, the narrator, can picture these things because Rebecca West could, because any English civilian could by 1916. From the war's beginning, its terrible particulars were brought home continually to England and into the lives and minds of people there. The First World War was the first English war to be reported and photographed in daily newspapers, and the first to be filmed and shown to the public in cinemas. It was also the first English war to be fought by middle-class and upper-class volunteers, men who could read and write, and so could describe the war in their letters, and would talk about it to women like Jenny when they returned on leave. Jenny has seen the war "on the war-films," and has heard the black jokes that soldiers make (*"I've got no legs!. . . . I've got no hands!"*), and the stories they tell. She doesn't know the whole story of the war, but she knows the worst of it—the horror stories that we all have in our heads, and visualize as the reality of the Western Front. Such knowledge would not have been available to a sheltered woman like Jenny during any previous English war: this was the first war that women *could* imagine, and so it was the first that a woman could write into a novel.

The Return of the Soldier, then, is a novel of an enclosed world invaded by public events, a private novel containing history. But not only war history. The time of the present action is wartime, 1916, but there is another date in the book, too—1901, the last time that Chris, the returned soldier, can remember. That date is carefully and precisely chosen. It is the year Queen Victoria died and her son Edward succeeded to the throne, and gave his name to the decade that followed. Part of the novel is Edwardian.

The Edwardian years were a turbulent time in English history, a narrow channel where the tides of Victorianism and Modernism met. English wealth was never more ostentatious than at that time, nor English poverty deeper. There were troubles with workers, women, and the Irish; political and social powers shifted. And then there was the great trouble of the War. Those troubles, endured together, made England seem a different place, cut off from its own past as by a breach in time.

Chris Baldry's shell-shocked amnesia has erased those

troubled years. He remembers only the time before all the changes, when he was happy. His suffering mind has retreated from war and history into a romantic dream of Monkey Island, where he first met Margaret; there, in his mind, time is stopped and love is changeless. "It was strange," Jenny thinks, "that both Chris and she spoke of it as though it were not a place, but a magic state which largely explained the actions performed in it." And so it is, for them. But it isn't the only romantic dream place in the novel; there is also England, the pastoral, unchanging England of which Baldry Court is the embodiment. That, too, is a dream, from which the war must be the awakening.

Jenny, looking back, recalls how change entered the dream world of the lovers and drew them into history, how Chris was compelled by family necessities to become a modern man of business; how he married Kitty, the sort of woman such a man does marry; how the family house, which in its original state had stood for the old dream of England, was remade into a sterile modern place; and how Margaret married an ineffectual working man and settled into bleak and shabby poverty.

One might read the lovers' story as an analogue in the private world of England's story over those fifteen Edwardian years. Something that seemed changeless changed; a dream of England, and of happiness and peace, was lost. Chris's amnesia has taken him back to the time before change; other Englishmen yearned back, too, to an innocent, unspoiled England that had not been lost, not because of the war alone, but because of the whole disfiguring process of modern change.

You find that sense of the disfigurement of England in Jenny's thoughts, as she considers the town where Margaret lives:

Wealdstone. That is the name of the red suburban stain which fouls the fields three miles nearer London than Harrowweald. One cannot now protect one's environment as one could in the old days.

And later:

> Wealdstone is not, in its way, a bad place; it lies in the lap
> of open country and at the end of every street rise the green
> hill of Harrow and the spires of Harrow School. But all the
> streets are long and red and freely articulated with railway
> arches, and factories spoil the skyline with red angular
> chimneys, and in front of the shops stand little women with
> backs ridged by cheap stays, who tapped their upper lips
> with their forefingers and made other feeble, doubtful ges-
> tures as though they wanted to buy something and knew that
> if they did they would have to starve some other appetite.

In this dreary scene, change and poverty and ugliness meet and
confirm each other.

Wealdstone is not merely one imagined town: it is every place
on our planet where the sprawl of industrialism has invaded
the natural world. And it is not a matter of landscape only; in
these ugly places people are made ugly by the lives they lead.
Those ugly lives in ugly places touched the imagination of other
writers in this century's early years. Readers of E. M. Forster's
Howard's End will remember the "red rust" that he saw creep-
ing out from London, staining the countryside. D. H. Lawrence
saw it, too, and put it into his novels, into *The Rainbow* and
Women in Love. That idea wasn't new in this century; Victorian
social critics had worried over the division of England into two
nations, one rich, one poor, and the creation of industrial blight
where there had once been beauty. Forster and Lawrence and
Rebecca West continued this tradition: they looked around at
ruined landscapes and stunted lives, and made the Uglification
of England their theme.

In the private space of *The Return of the Soldier*, the two
nations of England are represented by two women: Kitty, who
is beautiful and rich; and Margaret, who is made ugly by her

poverty. We see them as the observant Jenny sees them, as the sums of their material conditions; her observations of their clothes, their houses, their furniture are exact, fastidious, and relentless. Kitty, among the "brittle beautiful things" she owns, is a part of the décor, elegant and cared for like a work of art or an expensive piece of furniture. This is how Jenny sees her, dressed to dine with her husband on the first night of his return:

> Around her throat were her pearls, and her longer chain of diamonds dropped, looking cruelly bright, to her white small breasts; because she held some needle-work to her bosom I saw that her right hand was stiff with rings and her left hand bare save for her wedding-ring. . . . There were green curtains close by, and now the lights on her satin gown were green like cleft ice. She looked as cold as moonlight, as virginity, but precious; the falling candlelight struck her hair to bright, pure gold.

Decorated and cold, she sits in a luxurious place and waits. The whole scene is like a colored photograph in some glossy women's magazine.

And here is Margaret, as Jenny sees her at home:

> As I spoke . . . I turned my eyes away from her, because she was sitting on a sofa, upholstered in velveteen of a sickish green, which was so low that her knees stuck up in front of her and she had to clasp them with her seamed floury hands; and I could see that the skin of her face was damp. . . . She drew one of those dreadful hands across her tears, her damp skin, her rough, bagging overall. "I'm hot. I've been baking. You can't get a girl nowadays that understands the baking."

Kitty is a beautiful object among beautiful objects; Margaret is a worn working-class woman on a hideous sofa in a dismal house. Rebecca West had learned already that our dwelling places are stage sets that we create out of what life gives us, and that, once created, they define and shape the lives we live there. Perhaps she had learned that lesson from Henry James, about whom she had just written a clever, impertinent book; his *Spoils of Poynton* hovers over Baldry Court.

But she also had learned another truth somewhere else, perhaps from life: that beauty is only aesthetic, and that it is unimportant, compared to love. Margaret, with her worn hands and her dowdy hat, makes that truth evident: how unconcerned with the merely beautiful love is, how plain, how worn, yet how protective and enveloping it can be. And, in its way, how beautiful.

The insistent presence of the beauty of wealth and the ugliness of poverty makes *The Return of the Soldier* a novel about class and the class structure of English society. Observations about class are scattered through it: how the rich hate the poor, how the poor are afraid of menservants. And class truths are demonstrated in the relations between the two principal women: Kitty uses her manners to reject and wound; Margaret, who has no manners, is simply kind and sympathetic by instinct. There is a political point here, too; Rebecca West when young declared herself a Socialist, and it is clear in the novel that she valued the feeling life of the poor, and despised the rich, insulated from feeling by their possessions and their breeding.

Rebecca West calibrates her classes with a delicate awareness of the structure of the system. Class in England at the beginning of the twentieth century was a complex system of many fine distinctions (and still is, for that matter). One might talk as though there were only three classes—upper, middle, and lower—but in fact within each class there were qualifications and subdivisions that a keen social observer would recognize at once. (George Orwell, for example, decided that he had been born into "the lower-upper-middle class.") Chris Baldry is upper-class, and lives in a country house that is both large and handsome; yet he isn't "county," that is, he isn't one of the old landowning gentry. In peacetime, he paid for his expensive life by working in London in the family business (something to do with Mexican mines; Jenny is vague on men's-world details). He is a country gentleman of a new Edwardian kind, with his financial roots in the City—a member, Orwell might have said, of the lower-upper class.

Kitty, his wife, is another Edwardian type. We learn nothing of her history: she has no past, no family, no inherited place in society; she is simply an expensive woman who knows the rules of her wealthy class, which is not so much *upper* as simply *rich*. Margaret, Kitty's opposite, is of the lower class, but not the lowest level of that class; she has a daily help, and she carries calling cards (slum-dwellers don't do that). She is upper-lower class; but she is close enough to the low end of the poverty scale to be soiled by it—"seamed and scored and ravaged by squalid circumstances," Jenny says.

These are not the conventional classes of the old, stable England; they are the shifting, insecure classes of a society in change, where money rules and anyone may sink into another, poorer class at any time. By observing class in such precise and immediate terms, Rebecca West made her novel historical in a broader sense than its wartime setting would suggest.

The Return of the Soldier is a love story, with a conventional love story plot: a man must choose between two women—one warm and loving, the other cold and narcissistic. It seems an easy choice: choose love. The particular wartime circumstances of the story make the choice seem even easier. If Chris chooses Margaret, he will be withheld from the war; if he chooses Kitty, he will be ordered back to the Front, to suffering and possible death: so choose life. But in fact the choice is not his to make: shell shock has deprived him of the capacity to choose. He moves aimlessly through the novel in the passive state of someone for whom things must be done, and decisions made—like a patient in a hospital, or a small child. His destiny is in the hands of the women.

There is, to be sure, an external agent of change—the psychiatrist, Dr. Anderson. In her use of a psychiatrist in wartime, Rebecca West was being very up-to-date, for the idea that war might cause mental illness in soldiers, who would have to be given psychiatric treatment, was only beginning to be recognized at the time she wrote. But psychiatry isn't really an issue in the novel; Anderson is simply a device by which the moral choice that must be made is dramatically set out.

That choice is a hard one, and *The Return of the Soldier* is a hard novel because it does not flinch from what the right moral choice must be, nor from what it will cost. Its hardness is forced upon us both by Jenny, the sensitive instrument on which the moral issue is registered, and by Margaret, who must make the choice, against her own happiness and that of the man she loves. In the stern morality of the novel, the choice of love and life is wrong, not because coldness and death are right, but because the true opposites of love, in this case, are reality and truth.

Reality and truth are the hard, inexorable words of the novel. Because, as Margaret says, "the truth's the truth," Chris must be forced out of his happy dream of the past into the present. The agent of his return must be Margaret, who alone has the power to force him to reenter reality. But it is Jenny who will formulate the moral principle that makes that action necessary and right:

There is a draught that we must drink or not be fully human. . . . I knew that one must know the truth. I knew quite well that when one is adult one must raise to one's lips the wine of the truth, heedless that it is not sweet like milk but draws the mouth with its strength, and celebrate communion with reality, or else walk for ever queer and small like a dwarf.

And so the novel's title becomes, in the end, a bitter irony: the soldier, who returned from war and suffering to remembered happiness, must return again to reality—to 1916, his wife, his war—because it *is* reality. The cost is high: he must become once more "every inch a soldier." But not to return, not to be cured of his happiness, would be worse; left as he was, he would not be quite a man.

The Return of the Soldier ends where it began, in the reality of 1916, and that gives the ending a special quality, which shouldn't be overlooked. A novel about a war, written during the war, cannot have the kind of completion that historical novels usually have; the critical action in the world, the war itself, doesn't yet have an ending, has not been won or lost. And because that is the case, the end of the novel is not a tidy termination, but a precipice over which Chris must step into the terrible ordeal of war. We know that ordeal awaits him; and so do the women who conspire to return him to it. The truths of history must be added to the costs of choosing reality.

It is a harsh moral lesson that this novel teaches. It says that Reality is the highest human value—higher than love, higher than happiness, and that not to accept and honor that high value is to be less than human. Rebecca West did honor reality, and all her life made it the ruling principle of her work. Her later books spread widely into history, politics, and religion; she wrote about crime and treason, and reported memorably on the Nuremberg Trials, and always with the same strict honesty. But the principle of reality was already there in her hard, delicate first novel, in the choice that one woman makes, and another woman confirms.

*

First published as an introduction to
Rebecca West's The Return of the Soldier *(1998).*

An Introduction to Graeme West

The Diary of a Dead Officer is a war-book that stands outside the customary range of literary genres. It is not a novel or a memoir or a book of poems; it is simply the surviving fragments of a young man's writings about war, gathered together as a stretcher-bearer might gather the dismembered body of a dead soldier. The book contains diary entries, introspective essays, a few letters, and some poems—the whole moving from the beginning of Graeme West's war to the end of it, but discontinuously, so that what one has is not so much a narrative as a collage. If it is nonetheless a powerful document, that is perhaps in part because of its fragmentedness: like other works that came later—*The Waste Land*, for example, and Ernest Hemingway's *In Our Time*, and even in its way Erich Maria Remarque's *All Quiet on the Western Front*—it offers an apparent lack of order that becomes a metaphor for the war experience itself.

Arthur Graeme West was born in 1891 in Warwickshire, the eldest son of a middle-class family. When he was ten, the family moved to Highgate, on the northern edge of London, and Graeme (as he was called) went to Highgate School there, and then to Blundell's (a public school in Devon). Graeme was a shy, unathletic boy—a "worm," in Blundell's slang—and he was unpopular and unhappy in school. But he was clever enough to win a scholarship to Balliol College, Oxford, and went up in the autumn of 1910. At Oxford, he read widely and indiscriminately, which made him an informed student, but not of the kind that succeeds in examinations; he took a third in Mods and a second in Greats—a very undistinguished record for a scholarship-holder.

West was happier at Oxford than he had been at Highgate and Blundell's, and even began to make friends, though his old school chum C. E. M. Joad did not find it easy to explain just what appeal he had. "When people were attracted to West," Joad wrote,

> —and as time went on they became more and more attracted— they would have found it difficult to say what is was they liked in him. He had no outstanding qualities to win you. He was not pre-eminently witty, generous, genial, or hospitable. He knew few anecdotes, and never told them.[1]

But friends did not seem to have been very important to him. He was the sort of young man who is happy simply being donnish: he read, he looked at pictures, he went on long walks, and was content if he walked alone. He was, in short, the sort of young man that Oxford was made for.

When the Great War began in August 1914, West had already completed four years at Oxford. He returned that autumn, intending to spend a fifth year reading English literature, evidently quite unaware that the war might intrude upon his life of books. But Oxford was full of the war: young men were joining up, men in uniform were everywhere, home guard units were drilling. He could not ignore it. By Christmas he had been

---

1. C. E. M. Joad, introduction to Graeme West, *The Diary of a Dead Officer: Being the Posthumous Papers of A. G. West*, ed. C. J. [C. E. M. Joad] (1919).

caught up in the wave of war enthusiasm that swept the country, and had enlisted as a private in the Public Schools Battalion.

It was not with public school boys that he trained, though: the fellow soldiers that he described in his diary entries of those weeks were obviously lower-class men. They had thick necks and flapping ears, he said, and dull faces on which he saw "insolent leering expressions," or "vaguely wretched stupidity"; and they stank. West hated them, and hated being an enlisted man: not surprisingly, the young man from Blundell's and Balliol was a snob. And a literary one at that: seeking for an image of his hateful fellows, he compared them to the Morlocks in H. G. Wells's *The Time Machine.*

But he was in the army in a time of war, and there was nothing to do about his distaste. When his unit crossed to France in the autumn of 1915, West crossed with them. He spent four months at the Front, in mud and stench and noise—four months of great discomfort, but apparently not of great danger, or even of much activity. During those months, he had time to read *The Faerie Queene*, the *Odyssey*, and *Tom Jones* (one wonders what his thick-necked mates made of his taste in literature). But he must not have spent all of his time reading; he was a good enough soldier to be sent back for officer training in the spring of 1916. He went determined that he would get a commission; whatever happened, he would never return to the trenches as a common soldier.

Officer training, by West's account, consisted of out-of-date drill practices and mindless discipline imposed by elderly officers, left-overs from other wars. West resented and despised the whole business, but he endured it, because not to do so would mean returning to the trenches as a private. He was commissioned in August 1916, and after a period of leave was posted to the Front, to assume the duties of a platoon commander. The Battle of the Somme was then in its third month, and West was

in and out of the trenches all through that autumn, often under heavy shelling. He emerged untouched. Months later, in
the spring of 1917, during a relatively quiet period of the war,
he was shot by a sniper as he was leaving his trench, and died
instantly.

That was West's war—undistinguished, with its share of discomfort and hardship, but without anything particularly heroic in it. Many ordinary young men like him must have had
similar war experiences.

But there was another war in West's life: the war that was
waged in his mind between participation in the fighting and
opposition to it.

According to Joad's introduction, West had joined the Army
"from a feeling of duty and, in the best sense of the word, of patriotism." West's own retrospective account is less approbative.
In his diary, he recalled what he had hoped for, at the beginning: "my old imagined glories and delights of the Army . . .—
its companionship, suffering courageously and of noble ne-
cessity undergone." That passage has the ring of truth: a desire
for glory, nobility, and the companionship of courageous
suffering—those were his motives, and the motives, surely, of
many another young man. Not patriotism, but a sense of the
self glorified by war.

The diary shows that such dreams of glory did not survive
long; by the end of his first year of service, West began to record
contrary feelings. At the beginning of 1916, for example, he
heard of incidents back in England in which gangs of soldiers
broke up peace meetings and his response was one of sympathy for the pacifists. He began to ask himself what difference it
would make whether England won or lost the war. And in one
striking passage, he seemed to gain, quite suddenly, a long historical perspective, in terms of which the war lost all signifi-
cance. "I have realized this for myself," he wrote,

—the absolute nonentity of everything that men hold precious. Even the decision of this war is nothing; what does England matter, or whether she wins or not? Any man of sense must subscribe with all his mind and soul to the cry of Ecclesiastes; when he goes to the British Museum and sees the meaningless lost-looking Thoths and Rameses, Sphinxes and mummies, he must feel that they are now nothing; when he thinks of the wars whose voice has come ever so faintly down to us from those ages, and of all the men and women of those times, he must understand that all existence from the earliest Egyptian dynasties and aeons before them, to the present day, and on and on into the future, is without meaning, of no absolute or continuous importance.

In his development from the glorification of war to the repudiation of it, West was influenced by two writers. The first was H. G. Wells. In the course of the war, Wells displayed contradictory attitudes toward it; he wrote the book that gave the war its greatest cliché, and its bitterest irony—*The War That Will End War*, but he also wrote, in a contrary mood, the bitter and angry anti-war book, *Boon*. It was a story from that book, "The Last Trump," that West read during his leave that summer of 1916, while on a visit to Joad and his family at Box Hill, Surrey. It had a profound effect upon him.

"The Last Trump" is not a war-story; indeed, it never mentions the war, nor locates itself in time at all. It is the story of how two young men in London find God's Trumpet in a junk shop, and contrive to blow it, and of the great, if momentary, effects that great blast has on the spiritual awareness of those who hear it (after which they sink back into their customary stupid, human ways). It's not a war-story, but a parable of the blindness of human beings that allows wars to be fought. "The world doesn't see," Boon says, and that is what West found in the story, the unseeing world that had thrust this war into his quiet life.

It is clear from the context in which West recorded his reading of Wells how important the story was for him. His diary entry is dated August 19th, two days before he was due to report for duty.

> I go to W ... [Wareham, a training camp in Dorset] on Monday. We read Wells's "The Last Trump" out of "Boon" on a hill. If the war were to begin to-morrow and were to find me as I am now, I would not join the Army, and if I had the courage I would desert now. I have been reading and thinking fundamental things these last few months.

The other writer who offered West "fundamental things" was Bertrand Russell. Russell had been much in the news that spring and summer: he had been tried under the Defense of the Realm Act for the crime of writing a pacifist pamphlet, and had been convicted and fined a hundred pounds. When he refused to pay, his personal possessions in Cambridge were seized and sold. Trinity College then withdrew his lectureship, on the grounds of his conviction. To West, Russell must have seemed the perfect intellectual hero, the man who had the courage to oppose the war, and to suffer courageously.

In the evening of that same day—August 19—on which West had read "The Last Trump," he read Russell, and with Russell's help came to a brave conclusion, which he entered in his diary:

> I stayed up late and read B. Russell's "Justice in War Time," and went to bed so impressed with its force that I determined to stand out openly against re-entering the Army. I

was full of a quiet strong belief and almost knowledge that I should not, after all, have to face the trial of entering a new regiment as an officer, and that Waterloo would not see me at 2.10 to go to W[areham].

In the morning, he was still determined; he would say to his family:

I have come to a serious decision, long thought out, and now morally determined on. It will influence me more than you, and yet perhaps you ought to know of it. I am not going to rejoin the Army. There is no object, except the gratification of senseless rivalry, in prolonging the struggle; it is beastly and degrading. Why do we go on fighting? I will not go on.

The next paragraph in the diary begins, sadly: "I really nearly did say it." Nearly, but not quite. Later that day, he decided to make his gesture in a letter to the Adjutant of his battalion. He wrote the letter, and then could not bring himself to post it. The next day, he tried to do it in a telegram, walked into the telegraph office, and bought two penny stamps instead. On the twenty-first, he returned to duty.

From his camp at Wareham, West wrote to Russell, sympathizing with the persecutions that Russell had undergone. "Of course you know," he wrote, "that such sane men as still live, or have kept their sanity have nothing but admiration for you. . . ." That was indiscreet enough for a newly commissioned officer to write to a convicted pacifist, but West went further:

I know that you must have many friends in the army, and are aware that it, too, contains men of good-will, though it is through it and its domination that England finds herself as she is. . . . [2]

West had set himself against the domination of England by the very army in which he had just been commissioned, and had recognized in Russell a mentor in pacifism. But he had only done so privately; in all his public actions, he was what the army had made him: a second lieutenant in the Oxfordshire and Buckinghamshire Light Infantry.

At the end of 1916 (in a letter dated December 27), West wrote to Russell again, this time from the Somme. He had been reading Russell's *Principles of Social Reconstruction*, and had been encouraged by it. "It is only on account of such thoughts as yours," he wrote,

> on account of the existence of men and women like yourself that it seems worth while surviving the war—if one should haply survive. Outside the small circle of that cool light I can discern nothing but a scorching desert.

By this time, West had abandoned hope of making a personal gesture of renunciation of the war; he would simply try to survive it, in the hope of participating in the reconstruction that would follow. "Do not fear though," he told Russell,

> that the life of the spirit is dying in us, nor that hope or energy will be spent; to some few of us at any rate the hope of helping to found some "city of God" carries us away from these present horrors and beyond the braver intolerance of thought as we see it in our papers. We shall not faint and the

2. Bertrand Russell, *Autobiography*, Vol. II (1968). The letter is dated September 3, 1916.

energy and endurance we have used here on an odious task
we shall be able to redouble in the creative work that peace
will bring to do. We are too young to be permanently damaged in body or spirit, even by these sufferings.

Russell valued West's letter enough to include it in his autobiography. At the end, he added this brief note:

From the Press:

SECOND LIEUTENANT ARTHUR GRAEME WEST, Ox-
ford and Bucks Light Infantry, whose death is officially an-
nounced today, was the eldest son of Arthur Birt West, 4
Holly Terrace, Highgate. He fell on April 3 [1917], aged 25.

This story of a sensitive man's failure of nerve, under the
pressure of family and society, is one of the most interesting
things in *Diary of a Dead Officer*. But it is not the only one:
there are also the poems. West was not a prolific poet; only ten
poems are printed in the *Diary*, and of those only three are war
poems. So it is easy to see why West does not appear in anthologies of war poetry, or in most critical studies of the subject. But
one of his poems in particular is well worth the attention of
anyone who is interested in the literature of the Great War. It
is titled, from its first line, "God! How I hate you, you young
cheerful men!" and sub-titled, "On a University Undergraduate moved to verse by the war."

The undergraduate in question was one H. Rex Feston, a student who had left Oxford to join the army, as West had, but a
year later. He was killed in action in January 1916, after which
his friends back in Oxford published his poems in a memorial
volume titled *Quest for Truth*. The book appeared in August
1916, at the time when West was struggling to find the courage
to renounce the war. Feston's poems, which contained lines

like "I know that God will never let me die," and "Oh happy to have lived these epic days," offended West with their Rupert-Brooke-ish romanticism, and with their ignorance. West's rebuttal begins:

> God! How I hate you, you young cheerful men,
> Whose pious poetry blossoms on your graves
> As soon as you are in them . . .

And goes on to oppose that false and foolish rhetoric with the language of the truth:

> Hark how one chants—
> "Oh happy to have lived these epic days"—
> "These epic days"! And *he'd* been to France,
> And seen the trenches, glimpsed the huddled dead
> In the periscope, hung in the rusting wire:
> Choked by their sickly foetor, day and night
> Blown down his throat: stumbled through ruined hearths,
> Proved all that muddy brown monotony,
> Where blood's the only coloured thing. Perhaps
> Had seen a man killed, a sentry shot at night,
> Hunched as he fell, his feet on the firing-step,
> His neck against the back slope of the trench,
> And the rest doubled up between, his head
> Smashed like an egg-shell, and the warm grey brain
> Spattered all bloody on the parados:
> Had flashed a torch on his face, and known his friend,
> Shot, breathing hardly, in ten minutes—gone!
> Yet still God's in His heaven, all is right
> In the best possible of worlds. . . .

West was being unjust to poor Feston, though unknowingly. Feston had been at the Front for only ten days when he was killed, and almost all of his poems were written before he had had even that brief taste of trench warfare. But just or not, West's reaction is a strong war poem that renders the soldier's world of ruin and death vividly, and does so in the same trench rhetoric that other, better-known war poets were beginning to use—the plain rhetoric that names the *things* of war, the wire and the mud and the corpses, without abstractions and with almost no metaphors. West is like some of the others, too, in his anger and bitterness, which in his case may go back to Wells; he hated Feston for his ignorance, and for his stupidity.

Like Feston's, West's book was a posthumous volume; it was edited by Joad, and published by the socialist *Daily Herald*. (It was also published simultaneously by Allen and Irwin in London.) That combination of radical editor and radical press suggests that it was more than a memorial: it was by intention a polemically anti-war book. Joad made that intention clear in the preface that he wrote for it:

> If its detailed realism serves to correct in some measure the highly coloured picture of the soldier's life and thoughts to which the popular Press has accustomed us, it will not have been written in vain.

But if that was the intention, the book failed: it appeared some two months after the war's end, and that was both too late and too early to be successful. Too late, because it was not quite a war-time book, with the authority that such books seemed to have while the war still raged, and because public interest came to a sudden end when the war ended. (There are many testimonies by soldier-writers of the impossibility of getting a book of war-memories published in the immediate post-war period.) Too early, because ten years later there would be a great revival of interest in war writing, and books like *All Quiet on the Western Front* would sell millions of copies, and even memoirs like

Robert Graves's *Good-bye to All That* and Siegfried Sassoon's *Memoirs of a Fox-Hunting Man* would be best sellers.

Appearing when it did, *Diary of a Dead Officer* was reviewed dismissively—the *Times Literary Supplement* was typical, head-lining its notice "A Hamlet of the War"—and then forgotten. To my knowledge, it was only noticed once thereafter, and then only to be once more dismissed. In 1930, when Cyril Falls published *War Books*, his critical (and polemically pro-war) bibliography of the literature of the Great War, he gave West's book this paragraph:

WEST, ARTHUR GRAEME. *Diary of a Dead Officer*.
Arthur Graeme West and his type are ill represented among those who have left personal records of the War, though there were probably many who felt like him of it. He suffered from poor eyesight and had a struggle to get himself accepted as a soldier. When he got out to France he loathed it all, less from hatred of war itself than from dislike of what he called "the herd" and the herd spirit. He had none of that protective armoury of callousness or use, which was so valuable to most of us, and his life must have been miserable.[3]

This is a perverse misrepresentation of West's attitudes toward the war, but it is accurate on one point: West certainly was lacking in callousness. So, I would say, were Wilfred Owen, Siegfried Sassoon, Isaac Rosenberg, and Robert Graves. So was poor Ivor Gurney, who spent four years in France as a private, and was driven mad by his suffering. Owen wrote a fine poem about that quality that Falls so valued; he called it "Insensitivity."

Diary of a Dead Officer did not become one of the memorable books of the Great War, from which later generations would

3. Cyril Falls, *War Books* (1930).

construct their myths of what that war had been like. It came too soon, and is perhaps too fragmentary and discontinuous, too focused on West's internal war, and too little on the particulars of the battles and the trenches. But it deserves a permanent place in the literature of the war, as a record of a sensitive man's defeat in a war that he came to loathe but could not repudiate. As Falls said, there were probably many who felt as West did.

*

First published in English Literature of
The Great War Revisited, *ed. Michel Roucoux (1988).*

The Odds on
Edward Thomas

"Tell us," the Editor asks, "what is so special about Edward Thomas?" Well, let's begin with some dates. He was born March 2, 1878. He wrote his first poem in December 1914. He died on April 9, 1917. So his poetic career began when he was thirty-six, and lasted for only a little more than two years. Surely no other important English poet began so late, or lived as a poet for so short a time, and these facts obviously affect his verse. There are virtually no juvenilia, and there's no development—the poetic sensibility, and the poetic voice, were already there when he began to write, and they didn't change. He saw only twenty-seven of his poems in print, and he was denied the poetic growth that comes from revising, and even from reading, one's own earlier work. He had just turned thirty-nine when he died, and I can't help comparing this brief life with the longevity of Thomas Hardy and Robert Frost, two poets with whom Thomas has often been compared. If Hardy had died when he was thirty-nine we would have almost no Hardy poems worth bothering with; if Frost had died at that age we would have only *A Boy's Will*. So the late, brief burst of Thomas's talent is the first special quality to take note of.

A second is that though he was a nature-writer, and had

written more than a dozen prose books about nature before he turned to verse, he was not really a country man—not in the sense that Hardy and Frost were. He was born in lower-middle-class south London, and had no real experience of the English countryside until he was seventeen, when he went on the first of what became habitual country walks. He went to the country, then and later, because he believed in "Nature"—believed that out there beyond the suburbs there was a benevolent, curative power, something that he could enter into, that would receive him and make him happy. This didn't happen—he never put down roots in one country place, and so far as one can tell from biographies he never found happiness. But he continued to live there, in one country cottage or another, and he wrote continuously about it, in a flow of nature books with titles like *Beautiful Wales* and *The Heart of England* and *In Pursuit of Spring*—books that were written too quickly and for too little money, and mostly over-written to suit English tastes formed on Richard Jefferies and W. H. Hudson. And so what had begun as a conversion to the religion of nature became a profession.

Described this way, Thomas's affair with Nature sounds like standard Georgianism—that fag-end English Romanticism that produced Gordon Bottomley and Lascelles Abercrombie and the Georgian anthologies of Edward Marsh. And certainly Thomas knew these poets, and even admired them. But he wasn't really one of them, because he came to know something that they didn't know—that Nature had withdrawn her benevolence, and Romanticism was over. The desire to belong in Nature might go on, as it did for Thomas, but it would never be satisfied again.

This sense of Nature lost is at the center of Thomas's sensibility, and appears both in the later prose and in the poetry. "I am not a part of nature," Thomas wrote in *The Icknield Way*. "I am alone." And in a poem ironically titled "Home":

This is my grief. That land,
My home, I have never seen;
No traveller tells of it,
However far he has been.

In other poems Nature is a secret to which man has lost the key, or a language that the birds know, but man has forgotten, or never learned.

Thomas seems to have felt this way—at least in his gloomier moments—all his adult life; yet he didn't try to put it (or any other theme) into a poem until 1914. The usual account of how he suddenly became a poet is that in the spring of 1914 Frost, who was living among the Georgians in Gloucestershire, perceived the poetry in Thomas's prose, and told him to write it in verse form. This is Frost's story, and there is no reason to doubt it; but it explains nothing: why did Thomas take Frost's advice? Why was he ready for it *then*? There are two possible reasons, I think. First, that summer the war began, and depressed the market for prose nature-writing. (One might reasonably argue that the nineteenth-century's religion of nature died on the Western Front, where there was *nothing* far more deeply interfused, and the fact that a man loved Nature didn't alter his chances of life appreciably.) Second, the possibility of fighting in the war provided Thomas with the first real alternative to his career as a literary hack, and so made profitless poetry seem a possible activity.

Thomas enlisted in 1915, and most of his poems were written while he was on active duty—first in training in England, and then in the trenches in France. Yet he is scarcely a war-poet in the Owen-Rosenberg sense; only a handful of his poems—maybe half-a-dozen—are explicitly about war. Most of them are about the natural world, and man alone in it, and it is striking that Thomas was only able to put his feelings about these matters into verse when he was leaving his country places, or had already left them for the war.

They are melancholy poems, most of them, because Thomas was a melancholy man. Jan Marsh's biography of the poet, *Edward Thomas: A Poet for His Country* (1978), relates many examples of his deep depressions, when the burden of hack work and poverty and family would drive him out of the house to roam in darkness, sometimes contemplating suicide. But these fits, though understandable enough, must have seemed to Thomas adolescent, unmanly, unworthy. The coming of war, and the possibility of dying in it, made his melancholy an acceptable state of mind, and perhaps released it into the poetry. Some of his finest poems—"There's nothing like the sun," for example, and "Lights Out"—are war poems in this tangential sense, that they are about an attitude toward death that the war had made poetically possible.

But all this, though it describes what was special about Thomas's poetic career, may not be quite the answer that the Editor asked for. What is special, then, about the *poems*? For an answer, we might best go back to Thomas's relation to Frost. That there was an initial influence Thomas knew perfectly well; but it was one that he immediately set about to remove. In March 1915, three months after Thomas had written his first mature poem, he described his poems in a letter to John Freeman: "since the first take off they haven't been Frosty very much or so I imagine and I have tried as often as possible to avoid the facilities offered by blank verse and I try not to be too long. . . ." He had tried and quickly turned away from "Frosty" blank-verse narratives: he seems to have recognized at once that though he could speak of country things, he could not assume a country voice. One might make a basic distinction between the two poets by saying that Frost was a *country* poet, whereas Thomas was a *nature* poet. The difference is in the last lines of Frost's "The Need of Being Versed in Country Things":

> One has to be versed in country things
> Not to believe the phoebes wept.

Well, Thomas was the sort of poet who *did* believe that the phoebes wept, though he could not understand what they said. This is not, I think, an inferior state of poetic mind to that of the country poet—it is only a *different* one. Thomas was a natural Romantic, born in the wrong place at the wrong time, and aware that he was. His sensibility was softer, and more melancholy than Frost's was, with none of Frost's fierceness. It won't do to dismiss him as like Frost, only not so good: there's not much in his *Collected Poems* (see R. George Thomas's edition, 1987) that one is likely to mistake for Frost.

One is not likely to mistake him for Hardy, either; but Hardy's influence on him was surely as strong as Frost's. Thomas was one of the best early critics of Hardy's verse, perhaps because he found in it a quality that his own also has: it was, he said, "full if not of magic yet of a deep and strong suggestion of something which the intellect alone cannot handle." Hardy's Nature, like Thomas's, keeps its secrets.

Thomas's poetic characteristics—to turn at last to particulars—are, I think, mainly these: in manner, plainness, reticence, and sometimes a considerable awkwardness (such as one finds in Hardy sometimes but never in Frost); in tone, melancholy; in theme, a regret that is beyond the personal, regret for man's lost link with nature.

First, the plainness: like Hardy and Frost, he is best when he is plainest, closest to speech rhythms and ordinary syntax. Frost recalled that he had referred Thomas "to paragraphs in his book *In Pursuit of Spring* and told him to write it in verse form in exactly the same cadence," and Thomas described his first attempts to do so as "like quintessences of the best parts of my prose-books—not much sharper or more intense, but I hope a little." Poetry, he thought, should be "better than prose," but not different in syntax or diction. An example is "The Pond":

> Bright clouds of may
> Shade half the pond.
> Beyond,
> All but one bay
> Of emerald
> Tall reeds
> Like criss-cross bayonets
> Where a bird once called,
> Lies bright as the sun.
> No one heeds.
> The light wind frets
> And drifts the scum
> Of may-blossom.
> Till the moorhen calls
> Again
> Naught's to be done
> By birds or men.
> Still the may falls.

How could it be plainer, in language or in straightforward structure? Or more exact in its particulars? But there is, presumably, a difference between plainness and *mere* plainness, something "sharper and more intense" that we recognize in the real thing. Thomas gets that, I think, with the play of shadow and sun working with the play of present and past, with the *tempo rubato* of the varied line-lengths, and with the slow cadences of the two one-line, monosyllabic sentences at middle and end.

"The Pond" will also do as an example of his reticence, which saves his melancholy from falling into sentimentality and self-pity. This is a poem of loss, but so muted, and so emptied of the personal, as to be no more than an emblem of regret. (For another excellent example, see "It Rains," where the flowers of wild parsley seen at twilight carry all the weight of remembered happiness.)

Awkwardness? There are many examples. One might attribute them to the fact that Thomas's sensibility and power were developed beyond the technique that time allowed him. Or one might argue that his determination to eliminate from his verse the Pateresque, period-piece manner that much of his descriptive prose had, led him to be awkward in order to avoid being pretty. Most of the awkwardnesses are inversions like "All that the ring-doves say, far leaves among, / Brims my mind with content thus still to lie." They are, on the whole, less noticeable, and less objectionable, than those contrary cases where the easy lyricism and poetic diction of the prose remains.

Melancholy, the characteristic Thomas tone, is everywhere—in "The Pond," above, for example. It is not usually a self-regarding melancholy, though; consider, for example, how the personal tone turns outward in "The Owl":

> Downhill I came, hungry, and yet not starved;
> Cold, yet had heat within me that was proof
> Against the North wind; tired, yet so that rest
> Had seemed the sweetest thing under a roof.
>
> Then at the inn I had food, fire, and rest,
> Knowing how hungry, cold, and tired was I.
> All of the night was quite barred out except
> An owl's cry, a most melancholy cry
>
> Shaken out long and clear upon the hill,
> No merry note, nor cause of merriment,
> But no one telling me plain what I escaped
> And others could not, that night, as in I went.

And salted was my food, and my repose,
Salted and sobered, too, by the bird's voice
Speaking for all who lay under the stars,
Soldiers and poor, unable to rejoice.

A poem about melancholy, yes—the *world's* melancholy—as Thomas saw the world. But the presence of soldiers in the last line makes it *also* a war-poem. Just barely, you might say; but when you read the poem over again you see that the fact of the war, and of troops in the trenches, unable to rejoice, confirms Thomas's melancholy mood, makes it inevitable in war-time—and true.

Thomas has not had much recognition in the United States—no doubt because one Frost seems enough for us. But to the extent that he was *not* a plainer and lesser Frost, he merits our attention. For of all the Georgians he had the clearest sense of what a nature-poem *could* be in the twentieth century, and the truest personal voice. Like Ivor Gurney (another marvelous, neglected poet of that generation) he has been smothered by War Poets, because he happened also to be a poet who was a soldier, and was killed in action. It seems high time to give him his due.

In a letter to Frost dated March 6, 1917, Thomas wrote: "I should like to be a poet, just as I should like to live, but I know as much about my chances in either case, and I don't really trouble about either." A month later a German shell removed the odds on his life. But it seems clear to me that Thomas's permanent survival as an important English poet of his generation is certain. And that war-poet will be part of his reputation.

*

First published in Poetry *(March 1980).*

E. E. Cummings's
The Enormous Room

When *The Enormous Room* first appeared, the First World War was less than four years in the past. It was clear by then that the high rhetoric of wartime—the big words such as "Glory" and "Honor," and the big phrases, "The War That Would End War" and "The Saving of Civilization"—had been expedient lies; but the books that would refute those lies, *All Quiet on the Western Front, A Farewell to Arms, Good-bye to All That, Seven Pillars of Wisdom, Storm of Steel*, had not yet been written. The war, in 1922, was a ruination waiting for its story. For wars do not compose their own inherent meanings: a war is a tangle of terrible events from which meaning must be constructed by witnesses who survive.

Ever since that first appearance, E. E. Cummings's book has been considered one of the truth-constructing narratives, an indictment of the war and the governments that waged it, told by a man who was there. Writers of the classic war narratives took it to belong to their category: T. E. Lawrence called it "one of the very best of the war-books," and Robert Graves praised its historical truth. Today, three-quarters of a century later, it is still celebrated as a classic American product of the war.

That judgment is at once true and misleading. Certainly Cummings was one of the men who were there, if *there* means

France during the war years. But not as a soldier. He went to the war as a volunteer with the Red Cross ambulance group and served with his unit in the St. Quentin sector of the Western Front through the summer of 1917. It was a quiet sector while he was there, but if he had done his job and kept his mouth shut he would eventually have had his war, and his war story—there was plenty of fighting in the St. Quentin sector in the autumn of that year. But he didn't. He was a careless, insubordinate ambulance man, and he was a loudmouth. In conversation and letters, he and his friend William Brown were critical of the Americans and the French in the war and sympathetic to the Germans. To the French authorities they seemed possible enemies of La Patrie; they were arrested and put where they could do no harm to the war effort, in a French concentration camp at La Ferté Macé in Normandy. Cummings spent four months there; then, after appeals from home, he was released and returned to New York.

There is no war story in those events, not in the usual sense of the term. Where are the trenches and the bayonet charges, the artillery barrages and the gas? Where are the dying and the dead? *The Enormous Room* passes over Cummings's months on the Western Front in a page or two, beginning at the end of his time there; the story it tells is the other story, of his life as a prisoner. Surely the place for such a book on library shelves is not with Robert Graves and Siegfried Sassoon and T. E. Lawrence, but with the jail literature, with Fyodor Dostoyevsky's *In the House of the Dead*, Jean Genet's *Thief's Journal*, and Brendan Behan's *Borstal Boy*.

And yet, Cummings's book *is* a war book, of a kind. If it isn't about war as it is fought, it is about the power that war places in the hands of men who command—the power to inflict their wills upon the powerless souls whom they control. Armies work that way in wartime—so do prisons and concentration camps.

Prison is also a more literal part of war and its stories. Nations lock up such of their enemies as they can seize, and men have written their stories of that experience; in our century especially the prisoner-of-war narrative is a familiar category of war memoir. And nations also lock up their own citizens—those who are opposed to making war, and say so; conscientious objectors' stories are common, too.

Cummings's book resembles both of those kinds of prisoners' stories, but it doesn't quite fit into either category. He was neither a POW nor a CO; he had not been captured, and he was not charged with or tried for any crime. His imprisonment was not a martyrdom to either a patriotic or a moral cause. The troops in the trenches had a song about that condition: "We're here because we're here because we're here." Cummings's situation was like that. And because it was, he could write a book that registers the spiritual conditions that armies and prisons share: the authority, brutality, power, will-to-compel of those in command; and the weaknesses, discomfort, degradation, humor, and will-to-survive of the controlled and commanded.

The Enormous Room begins casually and abruptly: Cummings and Brown (called "B." in the book) are already at the Front, and already in trouble. Cummings's life up to that point is not to be part of the story. But that untold earlier life had made Cummings what he was, and had brought him to the distressing situation in which we first meet him: in a muddy French village in the summer of 1917, about to be arrested. So it is worth knowing.

That story begins in Cambridge, Massachusetts, on a street not far from Harvard Yard, in the house of Edward Cummings, Harvard graduate and Unitarian minister with a church in Boston's Back Bay. Edward Estlin Cummings was born there, in 1894. Those particulars—Cambridge, Harvard, and Boston Unitarianism—define a New England world, a class, and a set of values and expectations. No collective term exactly identifies that background; *middle-class* won't do, nor *conventional*, nor *conservative*. Perhaps *proper* comes closest: E. E. Cummings was born to be a proper Cantabrigian.

To be born into that secure and upright world was both a privilege and a problem. Many doors would open to a young man with those correct credentials—doors into Harvard College, into Boston society, into a comfortable future. But if the young man aspired to be an artist, those doors would open in wrong directions. Young Estlin (so called because his father was Edward) passed through the first door—he went to Harvard; but he went rebelliously and came out a less-than-proper graduate, a reckless, untidy free spirit who drank and chased women and intended to be a poet and painter of the most modern kind.

Inevitably, he quarreled with his clergyman father, who seemed to the son to represent everything repressive and hostile to art and creative freedom. Sons often feel that way, and fathers suffer for it; in fact, Edward Cummings was neither a bully nor an insensitive man (though he had perhaps a bit too much of the pulpit in his personality). Strong and authoritative he certainly was; but he was also caring, intelligent, and endlessly energetic on his son's behalf, as his letters during Cummings's imprisonment show. Cummings knew this—there is evident affection in even his most outrageously rebellious letters to his father—but he also knew that he would have to free himself from his father's authority if he was to be an artist. In January 1917, he left home for New York and settled in Greenwich Village to become himself.

Cummings's rebellion was more than simply personal. It was a part of the rebellion of his generation against the restraints of the past: against parents, against governments, against family structures and sexual proprieties, against conventions, against traditions, against controls in general. Artists of his generation were discovering the art forms for that rebelliousness in abstract painting and sculpture, experimental fiction, free verse, atonal music, jazz, and film. Consider the American artists who were born in Cummings's generation of the 1890s: Louis Armstrong, Alexander Calder, Hart Crane, Stuart Davis, John Dos Passos, William Faulkner, F. Scott Fitzgerald, George Gershwin, Buster Keaton, and Cole Porter. All significant modernists, all innovators who led artists in their fields in new directions. If this list seems to go beyond the customary limits of high art, that's the point: in the young century, artists would find new resources with which to express their freedom from the past.

Cummings's first taste of life in the Village lasted only four months, but in that time he established himself as a modernist, writing the kind of poems that would make him famous (his well-known "Buffalo Bill's / defunct" is from that period) and painting abstract pictures. More than that, he became what he already was in spirit, a bohemian, living among painters and writers and sculptors who were making the new art and doing what they pleased. Cambridge and Harvard and his father's Unitarianism were all in the past now; he had accomplished his freedom.

The war in Europe had been going on for more than two years, but in the Village it wasn't news. Cummings's letters from those months have almost nothing to say about the war, except that he had no interest in it. Yet when the United States declared war, he was conventional enough to volunteer and was eager to get to where the fighting was before it was over. No doubt he was drawn partly by the prospect of excitement and danger, as young men have always been, but the idea of Europe must also have lured him—especially of Paris, the epicenter of modernism in the arts.

When Cummings and his friend Brown reached France in June 1917, they did not join their unit at once; for weeks they lingered in Paris, being bohemian in the place where bohemianism was invented. They went to the Ballet Russe and saw *Pétrouchka*; they went to the Folies Bergère; they looked at Impressionist paintings at the Luxembourg; they walked the streets and sat in cafés and picked up two young prostitutes to share their experiences. It was only after five weeks of this life that they finally reported for duty with the *section sanitaire* at the Front. And there *The Enormous Room* begins.

The Enormous Room is like James Joyce's *Ulysses* in at least one respect: it draws meaning from conscious connections made to an earlier literary classic. In Cummings's case, the classic is *The Pilgrim's Progress*, John Bunyan's allegory of a Christian's journey from sin through tribulation to salvation. The links to Bunyan's book in *The Enormous Room* are numerous, beginning with the table of contents—Chapter III uses Bunyan's title and two other chapters ("Apollyon" and "An Approach to the Delectable Mountains") are direct references—and continuing through the book.

The similarities between a seventeenth-century journey narrative and a twentieth-century account of imprisonment in a concentration camp may not be self-evident, but some lines of a song from *Pilgrim's Progress* will help to make the connection clear. In the second part of Bunyan's book, a shepherd boy sings:

> *He that is down needs fear no fall;*
> *He that is low no pride;*
> *He that is humble ever shall*
> *Have God to be his guide.*

God doesn't in fact figure in *The Enormous Room*, but the state of being down and low certainly does. The book is a pilgrimage narrative, not in space but in spirit—a journey down into dispossession, to a place among the lowest and most deprived of human creatures, and to a kind of salvation there.

If you see the book in this way, then one of its most surprising qualities—its extraordinary buoyant tone—is explicable. For it is certainly strange that the story of an imprisonment in conditions of such privation and misery should be told so cheerfully. How *can* Cummings say of the camp at La Ferté: "By God this is the finest place I've ever been in my life"? How *can* he describe the desolation there as "impeccable and altogether admirable"? *Why is he so happy, where we would not be?*

The answers to these questions are in the shepherd boy's song, which contains the essential thesis of the book: to lose everything—all comforts, all possessions, all rights and privileges—is to become free, and so to be saved. He that is down is free from fear, from pride, from anxiety, and from the burden of material things, because he has nothing more to lose.

Being arrested for no crime provided Cummings an escape (that's his word) from the proper world of authority and rules and conventional behavior—from Harvard and Cambridge, from the Red Cross Ambulance Service and from the war itself. Stripped of all those social definitions, he was free simply to *be*. As the door of his first jail cell clanged shut, his spirits were paradoxically high: "An uncontrollable joy gutted me after three months of humiliation, of being bossed and herded and bullied and insulted [his version of his ambulance service career]. I was myself and my own master."

In that state of imprisoned freedom, Cummings tells us, time does not exist: "One day and the next are the same to such a prisoner, where does Time come in at all?" Prison events occur without connections or consequences: they simply happen and are over. And that is the case in *The Enormous Room*, there are episodes told, but they do not connect to make a continuous narrative. You could lift any incident out and put it back somewhere else and it would not affect the telling.

Instead of a conventional backbone of narrative, there are portraits. Cummings titled one chapter "A Group of Portraits" and that title would in fact do for the whole book; portrait making is a structural principle here—not the drama but the dramatis personae. Cummings's portraits-in-words have a distinctive quality that comes from the prison setting. Prison has stripped these people of their social identities (as it stripped Cummings) and even of the names that they bore out in the world. No one down here at the bottom has a proper first name and family name: instead, they have prison names: The Frog, Le Coiffeur, The Young Skipper, One-Eyed Dah-veed, John the Bathman, The Machine-Fixer, The Fighting Sheeney, The Spanish Whoremaster, The Baby-snatcher, Emile the Bum, the man in the Orange Cap, So-and-so (being a Turk), The Bear, The Lobster, The Clever Man. Imprisonment has reduced each person to a single attribute, as in a caricature or an allegory; they are not whole human beings but grotesques.

Cummings rejoiced in these grotesqueries, as he did in all individualities. But he also pitied them. These people, so reduced to their essential beings, had nothing to do with nations or politics or war; they were simply themselves and nothing more. Why should they be locked up? His political philosophy, insofar as he could be said to have any, is in this sympathy for what is individual, this celebration of each separate human being, each IS.

Of the portraits, four are especially important, and each has his own chapter: "The Wander," "Zoo-Loo," "Surplice," and "Jean Le Nègre." Cummings calls these four childlike men "The Delectable Mountains"—a phrase that requires some explication. In *Pilgrim's Progress*, the Delectable Mountains are elevations from which Christian can see his goal, the Celestial City. In *The Enormous Room*, these four men are inarticulate, powerless persons, but their essential innocence makes them saintlike; they give to the observing Cummings a vision of human goodness that is the book's moral core.

The Enormous Room has its place in the histories of war writing and prison writing. It also belongs to the history of modernism, and specifically to American modernism. T. E. Lawrence said of it that "the book is modern in feeling and new-world in pedigree," and on both points he was right. Its modernism begins with the date of its publication: 1922, the annus mirabilis of the modernist movement, the year of *Ulysses* and *The Waste Land*. Cummings had been to Europe; he knew what was going on in the avant-garde writing there. He quotes Ezra Pound in *The Enormous Room* and echoes *Dubliners*, and his book is full of modernist tricks—the linguistic playfulness, the density and compression of the prose, the odd allusiveness.

It is also modern in the multiplicity of its voices; like *Ulysses* and *The Waste Land* and the *Cantos*, it is a polyphonic work. Foreigners speak in their own languages, and Cummings himself speaks in many styles and vocabularies, by turns lyrical, comical, high-artistic, slangy, scatological, obscene—all Cummings, but also American, modern voices—various, conflicting, and yet comingled, like the nation, like the era.

Cummings was entirely conscious of what he was doing. In November 1919, while he was at work on *The Enormous Room*, he wrote to his mother:

> As for the story of The Great War Seen From The Windows of Nowhere, please don't expect a speedy conclusion or rather completion of this narrative; for this reason: that in consenting (it almost amounted to that) to "do the thing up" I

did not forego my prerogative as artist, to wit—the making of every paragraph a thing which seemed good to me, in the same way that a "crazy-quilt" is made so that every inch of it seems good to me. And so that if you put your hand over one inch, the other inches lose in force.

"Crazy-quilt" is exactly right as an image of Cummings's strategy: a work of art made of patches, all of them separate yet all necessary to the design. Consider, as an example, this Sunday church service at La Ferté:

> —And then one *Dimanche* a new high old man with a sharp violet face and green hair—*'Vous êtes libre, mes enfants, de faire l'immortalité—Songez, songez donc—L'Eternité est une existence sans durée—Toujours le Paradis, toujours l'Enfer'* (to the silently roaring whores) *'Le ciel est fait pour vous'*— and the Belgian ten-foot farmer spat three times and wiped them with his foot, his nose dripping; and the nigger shot a white oyster into a far-off scarlet handkerchief—and the Man's strings came untied and he sidled crab-like down the steps—the two candles wiggle a strenuous softness . . .

A patchwork of languages and characters and colors, of sermon and snot, a modernist painting (or better, a collage) made of sensations received.

But is all that French really necessary in an American book? Cummings's father didn't think it was; when he approved the copy for the American first edition of the book (his son was in Paris at the time) he allowed the translation of many French passages into English. Cummings was furious. "*Translation* of the French phrases," he told his publisher, "is, at least half the time, very confusing to the reader—it being very important that he should understand that a certain character *is speaking French* and *not English*." But there is more to it than simple fidelity to the fact; it is necessary that the book be a polyglot crazy-quilt of language because that was one quality of the experience, because La Ferté was a place where language separated human beings and left them isolated in their own inarticulate selves.

One of the languages in the crazy-quilt is Cummings's own: not English but *American* speech. It isn't always audible in the book—sometimes the style is simply standard English—but there is intermittently a voice that Graves, listening with his English ear, heard as the voice of "Cummings, the Harvard rough-neck." That phrase will seem an outrageous oxymoron to Harvard men, but the rest of us recognize what Graves heard: the slangy, wise-cracking, smart-aleck, rebellious side of Cummings, the side that got him into trouble with the French authorities. But it is more general than that. It is a characteristic American style of the time: you hear it in the writing of H. L. Mencken and Pound, in Damon Runyon, in Dos Passos. Made of cocky American self-confidence, aggressiveness, and strut, it is the voice of the new American wise-guy entering the twentieth century. Cummings was proud of that language— "the American language (sometimes called 'Slang')"—and so he should have been. It is our national contribution to the modernist discourse, and that is partly his doing.

Like all books that matter, *The Enormous Room* belongs to and lights up its own time, the years of the First World War and just after, when Americans and Europeans were trying to understand what had happened to them. What had happened to them was the first modern war—not only the killing and devastation on the Western Front, but the *spirit* of the war—which imposed a harsh, unjust authority on ordinary people in war's name and changed the relations between governments and people. *The Enormous Room* makes that spirit actual: how it looked, felt, smelled, tasted; it turns a great injustice into art.

For Americans, another thing had happened in those

years: many of them had discovered Europe for the first time. American troops had been there; they had seen France and they had been changed by the strangeness of "abroad." After the war, American writers and artists went to Paris, and their expatriate experiences changed American writing and American consciousness. In Europe, they learned what Henry James meant when he said that being an American was a complex fate. *The Enormous Room* is about that, too.

Modernism was also part of the change, and Cummings has an important place in that story, too. Early reviewers of *The Enormous Room* compared it not to other books but to popular art forms that were then emerging: to the films of Charlie Chaplin and the song-and-dance acts of American vaudeville. It was, they said, a work in a new manner: not simply modernism, but vernacular modernism.

Because it embodies these changes, *The Enormous Room* is a significant historical document. But a book that lights up its own time will light up ours as well. At the end of the Century of Modernism, Americans and Europeans will read this book for many reasons: for its extraordinarily inventive High Modernist style; for its account of a pilgrimage to life at the bottom, far below that most of us will ever know; for its unquenchable spirit; and for its celebration of human individuality. American readers will find something else valuable in it: an entirely American writer, speaking out of his American identity and his own American language. In his book we will find ourselves.

*

First published as an introduction to
E. E. Cummings's The Enormous Room *(1999).*

Cecil Lewis's
Sagittarius Rising

In the spring of 1915, an English public-school boy leaves school to enlist in the Royal Flying Corps (RFC); he's only sixteen at the time, but he writes and talks his way in. A year later, he completes his flight training and is commissioned, and in March 1916 he is ordered to a squadron on the Western Front. Over the next two and a half years, he flies various British planes on every kind of mission, in combat and out of it. When the war ends, he is twenty years old—a combat veteran who is not yet an adult.

In Cecil Lewis's flying world, everything is young, everything is new: the RFC has existed for only three years when he joins up; flying itself is younger than he is—only twelve years have passed since the Wright brothers flew their first hop at Kitty Hawk; the war-in-the-air is a new game that's still being invented. Designers disagree on how a plane should be put together; should the propeller go at the front and *pull*, or at the back and *push*? Should a plane have one wing or two, or maybe three? Should the elevator be put on the front end or the back? Should the pilot's central control be a stick or a yoke, or a steering wheel? How about handlebars to work the ailerons? Armament is another question that's just being thought out: a machine gun seems a good idea, but where do you put it so it doesn't shoot the propeller off, or pepper the wings with holes? Even the words in which they talk about planes are new (and mostly French): *aileron, fuselage, nacelle*; so are the words for the things you might do in a plane: *vrille* (to spin), *pique* (to dive), and *panne* (to make a forced landing).

In the course of his war, Lewis flew virtually every kind of single-engined plane in the British air service: the Maurice Farman "Longhorn," the Avro, the BE-2, the Morane "Parasol," the FE-2w, the SE-5, the Sopwith Camel, the Sopwith triplane—planes so different in their configurations that if you saw them parked together on a field you'd think they didn't belong to the same species. All of them have distinct characters and Lewis has strong feelings about them, as though they were fellows in his squadron—some likable, some cranky, some untrustworthy, some just dull. He despises the slow, clumsy BE-2 (it's unsuitable for active service, he thinks); he trusts the FE-2 (it's a sturdy, dependable friend); the Parasol, with its single high wing and no fixed horizontal stabilizer, scares him at first ("you had to fly it every second," he says), but he grows to love it and eventually flies three-hundred hours of combat missions in it. (He's flying a Parasol on the flight that wins him a Military Cross.) Every type of plane has to be flown differently, and Lewis describes each one as a working pilot would—the controls, the engine, how the plane handles in the air, what you can do with this one that you wouldn't dare try with that one. It's writing, you might say, from inside the cockpit, about experiences that are exciting, because they're new.

Newest of all, to a fledgling pilot like Lewis, is flying itself: to be up there alone, suspended in a fragile machine, with empty space all around you; to move in an insubstantial new world of clouds and sun and see the earth spread out below, a distant landscape that you don't belong to. The war is down there, you can see the trenches and the smoke and the exploding shells, and sometimes you will fly down into that uproar; but the air is your element, a different life goes on up there.

That other life is as much the subject of *Sagittarius Rising* as the war is; there are plenty of vivid descriptions of aerial combat, but there are also passages that are simply celebrations of the sheer joy of flying. Early in the book, when Lewis is still a novice with only twenty hours of flight time, he decides to see what a sunset looks like from ten thousand feet:

> I turned south towards Boulogne, climbing, always climbing. Already I was two miles above the earth, a tiny lonely speck in the vast rotunda of the evening sky. The sun was sinking solemnly in a black Atlantic cloud-belt. To the east, night crept up: a lofty shade drawn steadily over the warring earth. . . .
>
> The upper rim of the circle of fire dipped finally behind the clouds, and a bunch of rays, held as it were in some invisible quiver, shot a beam high into the arc of heaven, where it turned a wraith of cirrus cloud to marvellous gold. The lofty shade had covered the visible earth, and beauty lingered only in the sky.

It's a prose poem, made of sky and cloud and setting sun, and the pilot at home there, rejoicing in the beauty of his flying world. A reader will come upon many such lyric passages— about flying alone, about the beauty of the earth below ("how satisfying and permanent are the shapes of the woods and the pattern of the tilled and fallow fields"), about flying above clouds ("as far as the eye could reach, to the four horizons, a level plain of radiant whiteness, sparkling in the sun"). Such passages make the book more than a war story, make it a hymn to flying, a personal re-creation of a high emotion—how it feels to be alone in space in a plane.

Lewis began his flying career determined to fly the light, fast single-seater planes that pilots called *scouts* and later generations called *fighters*. Long before he actually flew one in combat, he imagined what it would be like:

> To be alone, to have your life in your own hands, to use your own skill, single-handed, against the enemy. It was like the lists of the Middle Ages, the only sphere in modern warfare where a man saw his adversary and faced him in mortal combat, the only sphere where there was still chivalry and honour. If you won, it was your own bravery and skill; if you lost, it was because you had met a better man.

At the war's beginning in 1914, that heroic, knight-in-armor kind of flying war didn't exist, couldn't exist. The planes the RFC had then were literally scouts; that is, they *scouted* the enemy, flew over the lines to see where he was. But they were unarmed; if you met a German plane over the front, you waved, or maybe, if you were feeling aggressive, you carried a rifle along with you and took a shot at it. Entire squadrons of planes designed and armed especially for aerial fighting had not yet been established or even thought of.

By the time Lewis joined his first combat squadron in the spring of 1916, new planes had been designed and aerial warfare had changed. Both sides had learned how to fix a machine gun on the fuselage in front of the pilot that would be synchronized to fire through the arc of the propeller without hitting the whirling blades. Planes had become weapons, and personal fighting, one man against another, was possible. And so the heroic dream could become real; in the air, at least, war would be romantic.

As Lewis learned, as they all learned, that didn't quite happen. Scout pilots might have their one-on-one fights, but most of their time in the air would be spent on less individual actions. Lewis carefully describes the ordinary, everyday kinds of flying jobs that pilots of his No. 3 Squadron did in the summer of 1916, while below them the Battle of the Somme raged: artillery observation, photography missions, contact patrols—none of them involving personal combat. The job of an artillery observer was to fly over a target that the big guns on the ground wanted to destroy and then inform the gunners where their shells were falling. The gunners would adjust their aim and fire again, the observer would report again, and eventually the target would be hit—at least in theory. A photography patrol would survey the complicated network of enemy trenches before an offensive. A contact patrol was a flight over the line during an advance, to locate exactly where Allied troops were as they moved forward (or retreated), so that the artillery would fire ahead of them, and not on them. All these patrols meant flying low over the lines, in the same air through which artillery shells were passing in both directions, close enough to toss a plane about in turbulence and sometimes hit it ("we lost many good men by direct hits," Lewis says), and within easy range of anti-aircraft fire and machine guns on the ground. There'd be plenty of danger but no opportunity for individual heroics.

Such an opportunity might come on an offensive patrol. These were flights over the lines with only one aim—to meet and engage enemy planes. Tactics at first were rudimentary—engaging the enemy, if you met one, would be a personal matter, a duel between you and him. But by the spring of 1917, group tactics had evolved, and many planes might attack many enemy planes in dogfights that would fill the air with diving, wheeling aircraft, and make death by collision as likely as death by machine-gun fire. Lewis writes: "It would be impossible to describe the action of such a battle"—and then he describes one in a long paragraph of plunging planes, crackling guns, streaming tracers, and pilots, "each striving to bring his gun on to the other's tail, each glaring through goggle eyes, calculating, straining, wheeling, grim, bent only on death or dying." And then the fight is over:

> In the pellucid sky, serene cloud mountains mass and move unceasingly. Here where guns rattled and death plucked the spirits of the valiant, this thing is now as if it had never been! The sky is busy with night, passive, superb, unheeding.

Offensive patrols were planned and scheduled, but it was also possible to go off alone, or with a friend or two, on a *voluntary* patrol—just going Boche-hunting, as a farmer might go off with his shotgun after rabbits. Lewis quotes a logbook entry from May 1917 reporting such an adventure with two other pilots, in which they attack five German scouts and score two confirmed kills, and another in July, in which he scores two more: altogether a "bag" of four (the hunting vocabulary is always there).

Combat flying is not a full-time job. A pilot on the Western Front might fly two patrols a day—one in the morning and one in the afternoon—totaling four hours in the air. During an offensive he'd probably fly more (Lewis says he flew six hours a day during the Battle of the Somme). The rest of the time he was free to do what he wanted. Lewis and his fellow pilots are curious about the front. On a day when the weather is bad for flying they borrow a car and drive up to the old front line at Fricourt, and from there walk on to visit a howitzer battery. They examine the abandoned German dugouts—how complete and elaborate they are, no wonder the place had not fallen! They see the debris that war has left—tangles of barbed wire, piles of ammunition, wooden boxes, torn tunics, overcoats. And smell it—dead horses, dead men. Maybe they talk to a gunner or an infantryman, one of the men who fight their war on the ground, and begin to understand how different a soldier's life is from a pilot's. When pilots return to their airfield after a patrol, their war is over for the time being, and they have a clean bed, a bath, a mess with good food, and peace until the next takeoff. The life of a common infantryman is quite the opposite—filthy and verminous, Lewis says, a life of bodily fatigue, exposed to the "long disgusting drudgery of trench warfare." The men who endure it have a kind of courage that he doesn't have, and he praises them for it:

> I can never honour enough the plodding men who bore the burden of war, who gave us victory (for what it proved to be worth) because they stuck it.

But pilots aren't plodders; they're a breed apart. "The R. F. C. attracted the adventurous spirits, the devil-may-care young bloods of England, the fast livers, the furious drivers—men who were not happy unless they were taking risks." Lewis saw himself as one of them, one of the wild gang.

When they weren't flying, pilots did what they liked. And because there were young, and male, they did what such young men do, wherever they are, what these same young men would have done back at Oxford or Cambridge—that is, they partied, they drank, and they picked up girls. But they did it with a special intensity because tomorrow they would go back to the stressed life of two patrols a day, day after day, until they were shot down, or crashed, or were sent home with their nerves gone. "Small wonder," Lewis says, "if, under this strain, pilots lived a wild life and wined and dined and womanized to excess": a wild life on the ground was justified, was necessary, because of the other wild life you lived in the air.

The party might be a night of riotous boozing in the Officers' Mess at the field, or it might be a "blind" in some estaminet in Amiens; or, if you were lucky, it might be a week "in town," which to English pilots like Lewis meant one town—London (Lewis never saw Paris until after the war). His recollections of a week in London suggest that what he did was customary:

> On my return to town, true to type and the tradition of the R. F. C., I plunged into a frenzied rush of meaningless "pleasure," which because of the sense that it might never be repeated, took on a glamour out of all proportion to its worth. Indeed today I cannot remember a single incident, nor face, nor word, in all that week, nothing beyond the vague feeling that somehow or other, with someone or other, I had a "jolly good time."

The someone or other has no face and no name: she is simply one of the girls, a necessary part of a wild party. A part, too, of a boy's eager, uncertain growth into manhood.

Two Cecil Lewises inhabit *Sagittarius Rising*. One is the sixteen-year-old who talks his way into the Royal Flying Corps, learns to fly and fights in the war, and returns at the war's end to the uncertainties of peace. The other is that boy twenty years later, the man who remembers the boy's war, and writes down the stories that memory tells him, and reflects on what those stories mean.

Memory is a lively muse but an untrustworthy historian; it selects and edits and rearranges its materials, giving them the meaning and shape that a story requires, and in the process turns bare facts into something else, something more interesting, more significant. Lewis the thirty-plus-year-old knows that and warns his reader in the first pages of the book: "Memory," he says, "that imperfect vista of recorded thoughts, eludes and deceives." And so it does. And yet . . . memories are the closest we will ever get to the essence of our past experience; not simply what happened then, but what it was like, how it felt to be that past self in that past life—what it meant to be us.

Twenty years separate the boy who flew in the First World War from the man who remembers that time. They've been busy years for Lewis: he has flown in England, traveled to China to teach the Chinese to fly, has stopped flying and returned to England to share in the founding of the British Broadcasting Corporation (BBC) and to work as a writer and producer there. He's been changed by those years. He's also been changed by events in the world around him. His book is datelined "1935–36": the middle of the thirties, the decade of the Great Depression, and of the rise of the European dictators—Hitler, Mussolini, Stalin, Franco, Salazar—a time when the threat of force grew in the world until another World War began to seem inevitable.

Writing in that dark decade Lewis can't help writing about *two* wars—the one that is past and the one that he sees is coming, interrupting his narrative of 1915–18 to brood on the world he lives in and on the war that lies ahead, as in this apocalyptic passage:

> But when the world did wake up to the dangers of the air, it woke with a shudder of horror. No wonder. Frontiers were gone. Security was gone. No man could hope for peace or prosperity under the threat of a violent death. The days of wars were over: massacre had taken their place, wholesale massacre of the community in which children would retch their lives away, women would be blinded, and men powerless to protect or succor. The end of civilization was in sight.

The war that's coming will be far worse than the one he fought in; nations will exploit the First World War's aerial tactics to destroy entire cities and annihilate populations.

With that vision in mind, Lewis looks back at his own war

and sees ideals there that have been lost. His breed, the pilots of 1914–18, had fought a war that was "more chivalrous and clean handed than any other." Flying, he says, was still something of a miracle then, and "we who practiced it were thought very brave, very daring, very gallant; we belonged to a world apart." All gone now, gone forever.

Nostalgia for that bright lost time and those heroic virtues colors Lewis's book. That's not a fault: memory is not a clear glass pane but a stained-glass window, through which we see our pasts more vividly. It's inevitable that a pilot, when his flying days are over, should look back with nostalgia to the time when he and flying were young, and the world was a better place. Lewis's ability to do so, and at the same time to reflect on both the bright past and the darkening world after, gives his book a binocular vision that makes it the profound and moving experience that it is.

✻

First published as an introduction to Cecil Lewis's Sagittarius Rising *(2014).*

The Death of Landscape

Everybody seems to agree that 1916 was the turning point of the Great War. It was the middle year of the war, and in the middle of that year the crucial battle began that changed Allied fortunes. The year had scarcely ended when the London *Times*'s war correspondent put his 1916 dispatches together in a book titled *The Turning Point: The Battle of the Somme*. "It is to the Battle of the Somme," he wrote, "that historians of future ages will point as the turning point in the war."

The *Times* man was certainly right—1916 was the fulcrum of the war. But the turning was a more complex and less encouraging business than he had imagined. After 1916 the war looked different, but not because a great victory had been won along the Somme.

The most striking turn, and the one that most affected the way the war was perceived (and still is), occurred in poetry and the visual arts. It happened in 1916, but not because of the Somme fighting or any other particular battle; it was simply that by the end of the Somme offensive, a number of young men who had gone to the war thinking that they were poets or painters had had experience of what this war was like for the men who fought in it. Many of the young poets fought along the

Somme; the young painters were mostly somewhere else. But wherever they were, they learned about war.

What they learned was that this war could not be written about or painted in the old ways. War was not a series of heroic individual acts, but a kind of machine that destroyed everything it touched—men, animals, equipment, towns and villages, the earth itself. To render it truly, the poet and the painter would have to turn away from glory and write about or paint the ruination, the unfamiliarity of war.

The turn in painting first appeared in a London gallery in the spring of 1916, when a young artist named C. R. W. Nevinson exhibited three war paintings in a group show. He had never been a combat soldier, but he had been on the Western Front as an ambulance driver and as a Private in the Medical Corps. He had seen no major battles and had not fired a shot, but he had seen the casualties and the destruction. He came back believing that "war was now dominated by machines, and that men were mere cogs in the mechanism," and that is what he painted. *La Mitrailleuse* (*The Machine Gun*) is a good example; one critic said of it: "This is modern war, the man a machine, the machine almost a man, no hint of humanity or pity about it, just war, the object of which is to kill."

In his first one-man show, in the autumn of 1916, Nevinson returned to this point of war-as-a-machine in several paintings and drawings, including *Column on the March* and *Troops Returning to the Trenches* (fig. 1), pictures of massed men in motion. The troops in these pictures move mechanically, but they are returning to the trenches, they know what is waiting for them there; so if these are paintings of machines, they are machines that understand and suffer.

Nevinson's show was a huge success: All of fashionable London came, every picture was sold, and the reviews were enthusi-

FIGURE 1. C. R. W. Nevinson, *Troops Returning to the Trenches* (1916). Etching. Bolton Museum and Art Gallery, Lancashire. Photograph: © Bridgeman Images.

astic. What the critics praised was just that mechanical quality that I have noted. One critic wrote:

> Perhaps unconsciously, Mr. Nevinson has succeeded in all his pictures in finding a symbolic equivalent for this war of vast and cruel mechanism. The soldiers themselves look as though they were the component parts of a formidable engine, drawn together by some irresistible force of attraction.

Clearly a change of consciousness had occurred. And that change was related to a new set of images: visual forms for imagining war in a new unheroic, antiromantic, mechanized way.

In the summer of 1916, while Nevinson was working on the pictures for his exhibition, a politician who knew nothing about art was organizing a government scheme that would have a profound effect on English painting. C. F. G. Masterman was a former Cabinet minister who had been put in charge of official propaganda. In the spring of 1916 he was visited by a literary agent (or perhaps by a painter—accounts differ), who remarked that the well-known etcher Muirhead Bone had been called up for the army, and that his gifts might be wasted in an infantry platoon. Masterman later asked his wife who Muirhead Bone was, and out of that conversation was born the idea of official war artists.

Bone was an obvious choice, even though Masterman had never heard of him. He had made his reputation as an etcher of views, mainly of historic European cities: he was good at drawing architecture and architectural ruins. He was also fond of landscapes, and especially of those that had an English look about them—views, that is, that remind him of the romantic landscapes that are the great achievement of English painting.

Bone was commissioned in August 1916 and went immediately to France. It is important, I think, that he went to war for the first time as an artist: he had not learned to see with a soldier's eye, as Nevinson had. He went in with the same spirit in which he had gone to Rome, and he found similar subjects: ruined churches and châteaus, poplar-lined roads, and distant landscapes with sometimes the smoke of battle on the horizon. He drew actual trenches on only two or three occasions; no doubt they seemed unpictorial to him, being so shapeless and so unarchitectural.

Two hundred of Bone's drawings were published, in ten monthly parts, beginning late in 1916—each part with an introductory essay and a commentary on each picture by C. E.

Montague (who would later write the bitter and influential war book *Disenchantment*). The parts cost a shilling each, so almost anyone could afford them, and for many English people they must have represented what the war really looked like. Bone and Montague agreed that what it looked like was England: the drawings and commentaries depict the war in familiarizing English terms. Montague's introduction to the first part begins: "The British line in France and Belgium runs through country of three kinds, and each kind is like a part of England," and Bone's drawings supported that idea.

Take, as an example, "The Battle of the Somme: Mametz Village and Wood" (1917–1918) (fig. 2). This is war-as-landscape, in the most traditional of landscape forms, the hilltop vista. The scene might be the downlands of Wiltshire or Dorset. The seated spectator (seemingly the artist at work) is a romantic convention—you'll find him in Constable landscapes and in Victorian landscape prints. He represents the viewer of the picture, who is simply another spectator, standing farther back. He confirms that what they are both observing is worth looking at, and that the right relation to it is a viewing relation: that's what landscapes are for. It is a drawing that has everything to do with landscape, and nothing really to do with the war being fought there.

Bone's pictures succeeded in England—that is, they achieved what the Ministry of Information wanted: they made the war familiar and they provided images of war that contained neither the dead nor the suffering living. But they failed in France. After the first two parts of Bone's drawings (titled *The Western Front* and *The Somme Battlefield*) appeared, the poet Wilfred Owen wrote to his mother:

They want to call No Man's Land "England" because we keep supremacy there.

FIGURE 2. Muirhead Bone, *The Battle of the Somme* (1917–1918). Drawing. © Estate of Muirhead Bone. All Rights Reserved, DACS / Artists Rights Society 2017. Photograph: Imaging Services, The British Library.

It is like the eternal place of gnashing of teeth; the Slough of Despond could be contained in one of its crater-holes; the fires of Sodom and Gomorrah could not light a candle to it—to find the way to Babylon the Fallen.

It is pock-marked like a body of foulest disease and its odour is the breath of cancer.

I have not seen any dead. I have done worse. In the dank air I have *perceived* it, and in the darkness *felt*. Those "Somme Pictures" are the laughing stock of the army—like the trenches on exhibition in Kensington.

No Man's Land under snow is like the face of the moon chaotic, crater-ridden, uninhabitable, awful, the abode of madness. To call it "England"!

What Owen is describing here—and by implication demand-ing of war artists—is a radically defamiliarized landscape, ab-solutely unlike England or any other landscape on earth. But he is also demanding that it be *moral* landscape, a new allegory of the evil, the horror, and the ugliness of war. You can see the problem for the artist: How is one to paint pictures that will be entirely strange and yet express moral judgments? It was a problem that Bone had not solved, and could not, because he had not been a soldier.

Bone had come straight from civilian life to his role as the first official war artist. Subsequent appointments came mainly from the forces: the Nash brothers, Paul and John, were infan-try officers in France; Wyndham Lewis and William Roberts were in the artillery there; Stanley Spencer served as a hospital orderly in Macedonia, and his brother Gilbert worked in a hos-pital in Sinai; Henry Lamb was a medical officer in Palestine. Some of them had returned to England as casualties and were sent back as artists (Paul Nash and Eric Kennington were two); others were simply detached from their units and assigned to record the war as artists (Lewis and Roberts); still others were commissioned to paint their versions of the war when they re-turned to England. Whatever the procedure, the result was the same: Masterman had gathered a group of war artists who had seen and felt war before they painted it.

By seeking out artists who had known the war, Masterman was shaping his war-artists program in two crucial ways. First, he was making sure that they would be *young* painters. Of the soldier artists I have mentioned, none was over thirty-one when the war began, and most were in their twenties; the young-est, William Roberts, was only nineteen. A few, like Lewis and Nevinson, had begun to make reputations before the war, but most had only recently begun to paint professionally. Because they were young, they were likely to be modernists—aware of the avant-garde movement away from literal representation and toward distortion and fragmentation of reality.

The movement had begun in France and spread across Europe in the years before the war. It had various names: cubism, futurism, postimpressionism, vorticism. Nevinson had been a futurist, influenced by an Italian group that emphasized force and energy, and celebrated modern machinery and the violence of war. Lewis was a vorticist—leader of the English movement resembling futurism in its love of machinery and destructive force, and in its use of half-abstract geometric forms. But whatever label they used, they all shared the sense that a radically new kind of art had arrived, and had made the past irrelevant and obsolete.

The second consequence of Masterman's decision to use soldier artists was that their paintings would draw upon direct experience, not upon the stock of conventional images of past military art. He imposed no limits on what that rendered experience should be: when Nevinson asked if there was any subject he should avoid, Masterman replied: "No, no. Paint anything you please." And so they did.

It is a paradox that though Masterman commissioned these experienced soldier artists to render the war directly, the best of their war paintings were not realistic in the ordinary sense. They went to work as war artists with two kinds of knowledge in their heads: knowledge of war and the fragmenting, mechanistic, reality-distorting vision of modernism. And they found that in the world of war those kinds of knowledge did not conflict. So Paul Nash, in a letter home from the front, could write: "I begin to believe in the Vorticist doctrine of destruction almost," and Wyndham Lewis, who had gone to France already believing in that doctrine, found that war, "especially those miles of hideous desert known as 'the Line' in Flanders and France, presented me with a subject-matter so consonant with the austerity of that 'abstract' vision I had developed, that it was an easy transition."

FIGURE 3. Wyndham Lewis, *A Battery Shelled* (1919). Oil on canvas.

A modernist method that before the war had seemed violent and distorting was seen to be realistic on the Western Front. Modernism had not changed; but reality had.

The pictures that these young modernists painted of the war are mainly landscapes—paintings, that is, of the earth's surface—but with fundamental differences. You can see those differences in three examples: Nevinson's *Over the Lines*, Lewis's *A Battery Shelled* (fig. 3), and Paul Nash's *We Are Making a New World*. Space is derationalized and defamiliarized in these pictures: the earth is seen from a great height, or from a position at ground level or below; the background is left empty, or disappears, so that distance doesn't run out to a horizon line but simply disintegrates.

On the earth, in these pictures, there are no examples of architecture, no aesthetically pleasing ruins, no signs of previous human habitation. More than that, there are no natural forms—no trees that retain the shape of trees, no natural bodies of water, not even natural shapes in the earth itself. In some of the pictures, human figures are altogether absent; in others they are rendered as insignificant or are distorted and mechanized. There is no appreciative spectator to these scenes, as there is in Bone's "Battle of the Somme." You might say that he isn't there because if he were he would be killed: but he's also not there because these are not scenes to which appreciation is an appropriate response.

Nothing in these pictures recalls the English landscape tradition; the world they render is beyond landscape. "No pen or drawing can convey this country," Nash wrote home in 1917.

> Sunset and sunrise are blasphemous, they are mockeries to man, only the black rain out of the bruised and swollen clouds all through the bitter black of night is fit atmosphere in such a land. The rain drives on, the stinking mud becomes more evilly yellow, the shell holes fill up with green-white water, the roads and tracks are covered in inches of slime, the black dying trees ooze and sweat and the shells never cease.

This is a very pictorial description, but it isn't a landscape; it is rather an anti-landscape, like the anti-landscape Owen described in his letter about Bone's Somme pictures. It is as though the war had annihilated Nature, and with it the whole tradition of romantic landscape, and had left an emptiness. (One of Nash's war paintings is titled simply *Void*, and his first postwar exhibit was called *Void of War*.)

The best of the English war painters solved the formal problem of how to paint the annihilated nature of war by adopting the anti-naturalistic conventions of modernism. But a further problem remained that was not formal: a painter might see the war as a modernist, but he could not help feeling it as a man. "I am no longer an artist interested and curious," Nash wrote to his wife, "I am a messenger who will bring back word from the men who are fighting to those who want the war to go on forever.

Feeble, inarticulate, will be my message, but it will have a bitter truth, and may it burn their lousy souls."

And how do you paint *that?*

Nash's solution was not a polemical one. He continued to paint his geometric, unpopulated war pictures, without visible anger or pity. But this does not mean that he was not painting his feelings about war; he was simply doing so in his own way. Before the war Nash had been developing as a painter of symbolic landscapes in the manner of William Blake and Samuel Palmer, and if you keep that in mind, then his trench-scapes seem bitter comments on his own romantic vision, and on the whole romantic tradition in painting, which the war refuted.

To make sure that his viewers did not miss his point, Nash began to give his paintings titles that bitterly and ironically evoked the lost landscape tradition: *Meadow with Copse* (a shell-pocked no-man's-land with a few shattered tree trunks), *Landscape: Year of Our Lord 1917* (where the irony is in both parts of the title), and *We Are Making a New World* (more shell holes, more dead trees, and a sun that rises from—or sets into— a bank of blood-red clouds).

Nevinson's solution was more direct. He began to do figure paintings that were not at all geometric or abstract or futurist— of a child killed in an air raid, a shell-shocked soldier, a doctor at a first-aid station. These pictures seem intentionally clumsy and representational compared with his earlier futurist paintings, but he considered them both important and new—not in technique, which seemed not to matter to him, but in what they said. Of *The Doctor* he wrote that "this picture quite apart from how it is painted expresses an absolutely NEW outlook on the so-called 'sacrifice' of war which up to the present is only felt by privates and a few officers who are to all purposes inarticulate."

In other pictures Nevinson focused on the noncombatants

at home and did satirical portraits with titles like *War Profi-teers* (two painted, overdressed young women, perhaps pros-titutes) and *He Gained a Fortune but He Gave a Son* (a portly man, no doubt an industrialist). These are pictures that express the soldiers' hostility toward civilians: in subjects and tone they are close to the poems of Siegfried Sassoon.

Nevinson did not abandon trench scenes altogether, but in the last years of the war he sometimes painted them in a more representational style than he had formerly used. That style got him into trouble in March 1918, when a new exhibition of his paintings opened in London. Among the pictures was one titled *Paths of Glory*, which was labeled and hung but which no one saw: It was covered with brown paper and marked "Cen-sored." It is a picture of the front as one might see it from the parapet of a trench—the shell-torn earth, the barbed wire; but on that dead earth there are two dead English soldiers. To my knowledge, it is the first war painting by an English artist that realistically shows dead men; not war, but what the dead really look like—a Landscape with Corpses.

Nevinson had committed two offenses in exhibiting his pic-ture as he did: He had violated a government regulation for-bidding representation of the dead; and he had also violated a regulation that forbade the unofficial use of the term *Censored*.

A few months later William Orpen, an older, "civilian" war artist, but a very good one, exhibited a painting of even deader soldiers—that is, of corpses in a more advanced state of de-composition—without any official opposition. But his picture was titled *Dead Germans in a Trench* (fig. 4). Apparently it was all right to paint the dead, so long as they were German dead.

In any case, by mid-1917 the Information Ministry had be-gun to shift the focus of its art program from propaganda to his-tory. In the last years of the war, these painters began to estab-lish a new tradition, as the war poets were also doing. There were publications of their pictures (*Modern War Paintings* in 1917,

FIGURE 4. William Orpen, *Dead Germans in a Trench* (1918). Oil on canvas.

British Artists of the Front in 1918) and there were exhibitions (Nevinson again in March 1918, Nash in May, Orpen in July). By the end of the war's fourth year, one could have seen, in London at least, a number of war paintings in the new tradition.

In these paintings one would have seen the end of two older traditions. The more conservative painters represented the end of the notion that war was a studio subject, based on slight observation or none, and the beginning of a new realism that came out of direct experience and did not separate the artist from the soldier. The more experimental artists recorded another ending: the end of romantic nature, and of its visual expression, the romantic landscape.

On the Western Front, Nature was dead—not simply in the sense that growing things could not survive the destruction there, but in the sense that the Wordsworthian idea of natural benevolence had died. And if Nature was dead, then landscape painting was dead too. The paintings of men like Nash, Nevinson, and Lewis are not landscapes; they are more elegies for the death of landscape.

What had happened by the war's end was that the actual experience of war by artists had compelled a turn of imagination—a turn that had necessary consequences for the forms in which the war was represented in art. If those new forms seemed modernist, avant-garde, vorticist, as they did in many war paintings, that was because the war seemed to confirm the experimental visions of prewar art. But they were modern in a different way. "There is nothing there [at the front] you cannot imagine," Lewis wrote to his civilian friend Ezra Pound, "but it has the unexpected quality of reality. Also the imagined thing and the felt are in two different categories."

The merely imaginary had become felt reality on the Western Front. The best war painters responded to that reality in ways that were like modernism, but different. The difference distinguished the soldier, who had been there, from the civilian, who could only imagine. It also distinguished the new war art from previous images of war. It was an art made out of ruined, disfigured Nature, out of ugliness; but it was something else—an art that testified to what war had done, to men, to the earth, and to traditional ideas of art.

*

First published in MHQ: The Quarterly Journal
of Military History *(Spring 1991).*

Verdun and Back

A PILOT'S LOG

October 13 / 10:15 A.M.: Shoreham Airport, Sussex.

The weather is with us, I think as we taxi out to the runway. It is a fine English October morning—bright sun, the sky intensely blue, with thin streaks of high cirrus clouds in the west and a mild wind blowing from the south. Visibility over northern France will be good.

We are setting out, my friend Anthony Preston and I, to fly the length of the Western Front from Ypres to Verdun. It's high time that I saw the actual landscape of the Great War, since I've just written a book about it; and because I was once a military pilot, it seems right that I should see it from the air. Anthony is with me because he loves to fly, likes France, and is better at navigation than I am. The plane is a Piper Warrior—about as fast as a Sopwith Camel or a Fokker triplane, though a good deal more comfortable.

I feel a certain astonishment that we have actually managed to get the project this far, and I half expect something to go wrong, even now. We had talked about such a flight off and on for a long time—where we'd go, and what we'd see—but in the idle way that friends do, over a drink or a meal, not really expecting that it will happen. But here we are, turning into the wind and cleared for takeoff.

Our preparation suddenly seems to me alarmingly casual: I have brought a couple of Michelin road maps, and Anthony has an air navigation chart covered with purple stripes that are restricted areas and circles that are radio beacons. And we have my copy of *Before Endeavours Fade*, the late Rose Coombs's wonderful guide to the battlefields, which we hope will help us to find the landmarks of the front when we get there. Anthony, being an ex-RAF pilot and accustomed to these air spaces, is jauntily confident: just up to Dungeness, across to Calais, and straight on for Ypres. A piece of cake, he says.

We take off to the south, and I find myself thinking not about the First World War but about the Second. The British commemorated the fiftieth anniversary of the Battle of Britain not long ago, and down here on the South Coast is where much of it was fought. Shoreham, the field we are leaving, was an air-sea rescue station, and over there to the west, under our wing, is Tangmere, a wartime Spitfire field. And below us is the Channel, where the unlucky and the unskillful pilots in that battle ended their shares of the war.

10:53 A.M.: Dungeness.

This is the point of English land along our route that is closest to France—about twenty-five miles. I bank to the right and head toward Cape Gris-Nez. I am taking the Channel! A commonplace enough thing to do nowadays—the air is full of stockbrokers flying their wives to Le Touquet for the weekend—but I feel an excitement, as though I were Louis Blériot, eighty-odd years ago. We're a little faster than he was. It took him thirty-seven minutes in 1909, crossing in the other direction, and we'll make it in fifteen. And we're a good deal higher—he couldn't climb above a hundred feet. But it's the same journey. The sea is calm but cold-looking, and as we leave the land behind I find myself listening to the engine with a particular attentiveness, as one always does over water. Freighters and tankers are scattered over the surface below us, and both coasts are visible all the way, so I don't feel any of the loneliness that used to seize me as I flew over the Pacific, when there was nothing but water down below. Yet I still have the uneasy feeling that there is no place to land. And then, gradually, the dark smear along the horizon ahead becomes a flat coast, and we are over France.

11:40 A.M.: Calais.

Calais Airport is just a bare, half-abandoned-looking field stretched out beside a long sand beach—one strip and a couple of buildings, one with a squat tower. The controller in the tower is bored but obliging; he directs us to the parking area in slow, careful English. The customs official is hard to find on a Saturday morning, but amiable enough once we locate him. One plane takes off, and its high-pitched sputter fades to silence. Nothing else happens. If limbo had an airport, it would be like this one, and we are glad to get back into the bright air, heading east for Ypres. Somewhere on this leg we will cross over Belgium, but we've decided not to mention this fact to the Belgians. Why complicate life? Anthony asks. After all, there is no dotted line drawn across the great plain below us to mark the frontier. It is all Flanders from up here.

Ypres appears as a round town, shaped by the canal that circles it. The ramparts by the Lille Gate catch the midday sun as we approach; in the center of the town the Cloth Hall raises its commanding roof and spire, dominating the lower buildings around it as it has since the thirteenth century. I know from the books that it was destroyed in the war, and that what I see is a postwar reconstruction, but from the air it looks convincingly medieval. The Cloth Hall was built as a vast covered market, but the market seems to have spilled out into the square outside; as we approach we can see that it is full of brightly colored stalls.

Anthony circles steeply round the east side of town, and I pick out the Menin Gate, England's memorial to the missing dead of the Ypres salient. I can see the British lion couchant on the top, and the long archway under which buglers still sound last post every evening. From the air the gate is solid and heavy-looking, but our altitude flattens it, making it seem less monumental than it must appear from the ground. One important feature of it is invisible to us: the interior panels engraved with long columns of names—54,000 of them, the names of the British Empire dead in the salient whose bodies were never found. But the knowledge that they are there, like an army of invisible ghosts, makes the massive architectural gesture of the gate seem grandiloquent, false to the real history of the dead. Men who fought in France felt that way about it. The English war poet Siegfried Sassoon saw the gate when it was built in 1927, and he wrote an angry poem about it that ends

> Well might the Dead who struggled in the slime
> Rise and deride this sepulchre of crime.

Pilots flying over Ypres in 1918 saw a ruined town in which not a single north-south wall remained standing. (The Germans had been shelling from the east for four years.) But to me, tipped up in a plane circling at 1,500 feet, it doesn't look battered; it doesn't even look restored. It is simply an old town, looking as it must always have looked. Only the gate—if you know what it commemorates—makes the war present.

North of the town it is different. At the war's end this was a dead, annihilated space forty miles square, without a tree or a house left intact. There are trees and houses here now, but signs of the devastation remain. Craters begin to appear, most of them filled with water and looking like country ponds, but more exactly circular than a natural pond would be. And the lines of trenches are still scrawled across the fields in white streaks of turned-up chalk that have not yet been erased, even after seventy years of plowing. Here and there, in the middle of a pasture or beside a road, are small military cemeteries, often just a monument and a few white stones, looking as though they had been dropped casually from a height and had fallen every which way. Their randomness offends the strict geometry of the field lines, and the whiteness of the stones seems out of place in the fertile green and brown landscape.

Poelkapelle lies just to the northeast of us, and because there is a monument in its center to the French ace Georges-Marie Guynemer—and because this is a pilot's pilgrimage—we fly over to pay our respects. It is another case of a monument without a body. Guynemer was shot down, and according to rumor his body was found by German soldiers and carried to a dugout; but the dugout was destroyed by the next artillery barrage, and Guynemer's remains were lost. The monument is easy to find; it stands like a hub at the center of the town's bustle. I know that there is a figure of a flying stork atop the tall column—the stork was the symbol of Guynemer's squadron and was painted on the squadron's planes—but from the air it is indistinguishable, just a black something. It might be a monument to anybody.

We turn east toward Passchendaele, a name that calls up terrible visions of a senseless slaughter. I try to imagine what the scene below me was like then, in the soaking autumn of 1917—the rubble of buildings, the smoke, the exploding shells, and most of all the mud, so deep and viscous that men drowned in it. But what I see is simply another tidy, prosperous-looking red-roofed little Belgian town, standing at the crest of a slight ridge in the midst of fields. The town is going about its usual Saturday business; cars are moving about and people are busy in the square. The land around it is dry and solid and well cared for, like any good farming country at the end of the season. It is all a picture of peace.

But south of the town, down a gentle slope, there is a large and unavoidable reminder of the war and its human cost: Tyne Cot Cemetery, shining white in the sun and visible for miles. It is geometrically ordered, with a vast neatness. From our altitude the separate headstones lose their individuality and merge into white rectangles, in strict order, like battalions on parade, forming one huge rectangle. Outside that parade-ground order are ranged other stones in other patterns, looking as though they had been added later by someone with different ideas of what the design should be. Along the front are a few stragglers, scattered as afterthoughts. Placed among the graves are monuments—a tall cross at the center, towerlike structures at the corners—that thrust up from the flat geometries of the stones and seem to govern the scene. In all that white tidiness are the remains of two cement bunkers, dark and shapeless.

It is the graves that impress me. The monuments say Not in Vain and Glory and Sacrifice. But the rows of identical white stones say simply Death, and Death, and more Death. The Menin Gate had uttered only half of that message to us. Tyne Cot tells it all. Around that pattern of the dead, the countryside repeats its own message. Cows are grazing in the pastures, a farmer is plowing, the fields are neat and ready for winter. The life of the land goes on.

12:45 P.M.: Ypres again.

We are headed south now, to find Hill 60 and Caterpillar Crater, where bitter fighting went on in 1915 and 1917. The site should be easy to locate: the mines that were exploded then left huge craters—one was 334 feet across in 1917. In this flat country the hill should be a landmark too. But we circle the hamlet of Zwarteleen for several minutes without finding anything; the hill from the air is no hill at all, and the craters have been overgrown by trees. In the end we have to do what any small-plane pilot does when he's lost: We follow the railroad tracks, and there, on the other side of a cutting, are the craters—one of them water-filled now—and the hill, pocked with shell holes three-quarters of a century old. This is a preserved piece of war landscape. Ordinary country business has not been allowed to enter it, except for a few grazing sheep, and the signature of war is still written on the earth. But the shell holes are closing in on themselves now, like holes punched in dough, and nature is slowly blurring the surface with grass and weeds. Like scars on a living body, these marks are fading.

A bit farther on is Saint-Éloi, and more craters, brimming with water and very pondlike. One is bordered with a line of poplars, just beginning to turn yellow; it makes a charming, very French-looking scene, like a Monet painting. Craters are all around us now, as we head on toward the Messines Ridge. Once more altitude flattens the earth: The ridge is not an escarpment, as I had imagined, but only a faint swelling covered by a dark line of trees. To the pilot's eye it is a landscape without significant irregularities. The infantry saw it differently.

1:00 P.M.: Loos.

We have crossed back into France, and continue south past towns that bear resonant names—Armentières, Laventie, Neuve-Chapelle, La Bassée—toward the battlefield at Loos. Slag heaps stand up ahead of us, conical gray piles that rise suddenly and symmetrically from the level plain. They seem to spread their gray deadness onto the fields around them. That flatheaded one over there must be about where the Hohenzollern Redoubt once was—the Germans' strongpoint in September 1915, tunneled and trenched and hung with barbed wire, hulking above the level ground. The position of the slag heaps may have changed over the years, but the basic landscape is the same. I try to imagine attacking one of those dead piles from the plain below, and I wonder—as I will many times before this flight is over—how men made themselves do it. But many men did: twenty thousand of them are commemorated in the high-walled rectangle of Dud Corner Cemetery. Some are buried here. Others are only lists on a wall. More names of the missing—this earth is full of them.

1:30 P.M.: Lens.

We pass over the dreary industrial city and head for Vimy Ridge. The Canadian Memorial Park there is another piece of preserved and reconstructed battlefield, bigger than Hill 60. Its craters and shell holes give it a strange look of abandonment and desolation, there in the middle of the tilled fields and the spreading towns. The Canadians have preserved and reconstructed stretches of trenches here, two twisted scars on the earth, facing each other across what seems an impossibly narrow space. They are cut so deep into the ground that even now, with the sun just past its noonday height, they are filled with black shadow.

They don't look quite like the trenches in old war photographs, though—more like models that someone might make who had heard about trenches but had never actually seen one. The Western Front at Disneyland would look something like this—so regular, so neatly sandbagged, so new-looking. But the no-man's-land between the trenches looks real enough. The overlapping shell holes and deep craters there have turned the earth into frozen waves, like a stormy yet motionless sea.

Across a valley to the northwest of the Vimy memorial is the village of Ablain-Saint-Nazaire. We swing over it, and as we pass I look down into the roofless ruin of the old church—the first ruined building I have seen. Above the town is the huge Notre Dame de Lorette French National Memorial and Cemetery. From a distance it looks like a shopping center on the summit of a hill, with large buildings at the center and parked cars in regular rows all around. The parked cars are in fact graves of all the French dead who could be identified among those who fell in the bitter fighting for the ridge in the spring of 1915. Those who could not be given names—another 20,000 men—are gathered in the central building, called the Ossuary. I think of the bones of 20,000 men, in one great pile. *Ossuary*. Bone house. An obscene term.

2:00 P.M.: toward Verdun.

We still have a long way to fly to our night's lodgings. And we have had enough of battlefields and monuments for one day. Anthony heads southeast, out of Artois and across Picardy and Champagne, toward Verdun. Here, out of sight of the sea, France is a spacious, fertile, and very peaceful land. Poplars along the roads and in the woodlands are yellow in the afternoon sun of autumn, and the light reflects up from the surfaces of little twisting rivers and straight canals. The houses in the village have gray roofs now instead of red ones, and there are more and larger woods. Cambrai is on our right, and Douai is to our left, but along our flight path there are no towns of any size. And no monuments or white rows of gravestones. War seems not to have passed this way.

Above the unchanging, serene landscape, we give in to the

simple joy of flying, alone in a high blue dome of air, the sun westering behind us now but still warm and bright, the earth stretching out to the horizon in every direction. A pattern of fields lies directly below us, losing its details farther out and becoming one blue-green distance until it fades at the horizon into blue haze. There seems to be no movement anywhere: no vapor trails scrawled in the sky above us, train tracks but no trains below. Only now and then white smoke rises in a tall column where some farmer is burning off a field. The wind drops as sunset comes on.

In all this emptiness, we begin to feel that our plane is not really moving, that we are suspended in midair above fields that don't pass by, above a river that is always the same river. We begin to study our maps, searching for railway lines, and check our watches. Where exactly are we? Anthony twiddles the radio, gets Lille, gets Metz, calculates directions. And then Verdun appears, dead ahead, where we had hoped it would be, a fortified city on a bend of the Meuse. It looks rather like Ypres (which isn't so surprising, since their fortifications were designed by the same man—Sébastien Le Prestre de Vauban, Louis XIV's favorite military engineer), but taller and more solid, rising from the banks of the river in a long, humped shape, like a loaf of bread. The end nearest us as we approach is green and parklike, with scattered official-looking buildings; this is the citadel. The far end is the town itself, dominated by its tall cathedral, with a tumble of gray stone houses running down steep hills to the fortifications at the base.

But just now we are more interested in the airfield, which should be over there to the northeast of the city. We find it, half-hidden between patches of woods, and head in for a landing. And for a bath, a meal, and sleep. It has been a tiring, moving, disturbing day for both of us—a long, slow flight across France, in search of a past war.

October 14 / 10:20 A.M.: Verdun airfield.

Our takeoff is a bit delayed—nobody works at the Verdun airfield on Sunday morning, it seems, or at least not until 10:00, when a man appears to fill our tanks and wave us off. It is another fine day, the sky clear except for a few patches of clouds far off to the west, and the wind out of the east. We will have a tail wind home, if it holds.

Passing Verdun, I look more closely at its fortifications and at its strategic position above its natural moat. It was a rock of a town that held out through those terrible months of 1916 and was never taken. Beyond the town on the right bank of the Meuse are steep wooded hills, where defensive forts were— Douaumont and Vaux, both eventually captured by the Germans, and Souville, which held out. The forts are invisible from where we are, south of the town and climbing, but I can see a tower on the horizon that marks the cemetery at Douaumont, and another ossuary. I know that the hills between us and the tower are still littered with the ruins and rubbish of the war— crumbling bunkers and gun emplacements, trenches, broken weapons, and, still, human bones. But the woods have covered them, and what I see are the green tops of trees, peaceful in the morning sun.

Even in the town there are no visible signs of war from where I am, looking down. Only the monuments, and most prominently the tall column that the French erected in 1920 to Victory. I had walked up to look at it the previous evening after supper, and found a plaque that described its unveiling. Among the gathered dignitaries, I noted, was André-Louis-René Maginot, whose line would contribute so little to the next victory.

Our first objective this morning is the Argonne—to have a look at the *American* war, I explain to Anthony. In a few minutes we can see the forest ahead of us, a thick carpet of trees stretching far to both the north and the south, and to the edge of our vision ahead. Below us is the Butte de Vauquois, a hill that was fought over by the French and Germans for four years, and taken by a Missouri division in a morning. It is divided down the middle by a line of craters left by mines that obliterated the village once standing on its summit.

We are once more in the landscape of monuments, almost all of these American, commemorating events in the autumn of 1918. They have an American boldness and scale, each one a huge memorial gesture. The village of Varennes is dominated by the Pennsylvania State Memorial, a large horizontal rect-angle of white stone, with a colonnade at each end—looking, as Anthony remarks, like a giant's bedstead made of marble. Across the valley on the Butte de Mont Faucon, the American monument is a tall Doric column that would be graceful if it were smaller. I feel a vague embarrassment at my nation's idea of commemoration, so huge and so tasteless. But does taste really have anything to do with what these objects attempt to express? Americans returned to Europe to fight in a European war, and many of them died. These memorials speak of a young nation's pride in its new role in the Old World, as well as of its grief for the young men who died here. Maybe size is the right expression of those feelings.

Beyond Varennes is the forest, dense and dark green, and scored by deep ravines. Down there in one of those folds, men of the Lost battalion were cut off from their division for five days, and I can see how that could happen. A tough place to fight a war, I think, as we float over the trees. There are few signs down below us that anyone did fight there; in a few years a forest will conceal the marks that entire armies make. I'm told you can find some of the deepest, and best-preserved, trenches on the Western Front in the Argonne. But not from the air. Only in occasional clearings do visible scars remain—uninterpretable lines, perhaps trenches, perhaps the tracks of vehicles. Or maybe nothing to do with war.

10:50 A.M.: northeast of Reins.

We are crossing Champagne now, on course for Albert. Anthony is playing with the radios, getting Paris Information and Lille Approach, determined to do a carefully navigated return flight, after yesterday's dead reckoning. So I fly the plane, just holding a heading, and looking down into the towns we fly over. This one has a massive cathedral, that one a football field, another an old bridge over a little river. Somewhere down there is the front that the French held, stretching all the way from the Swiss border to the Somme. I realize I know very little about this part of the line. The familiar names in *my* story of the war—Mametz Wood, Thiepval, Beaumont-Hamel, Lens, Arras, Ypres—are up ahead, along the British lines. My story is made out of the English versions, out of Wilfred Owen and Siegfried Sassoon and Robert Graves and Edmund Blunden. I know neither the names nor the stories of this countryside, and I peer down for signs of battles. At first there are none—it seems a country that has always been at peace—but further west, past Vouziers, the blotches and streaks of turned-up chalk begin to appear in the fields, like those we saw around Ypres, and continue in a roughly east-west line to Saint-Quentin, where they fade away.

11:55 A.M.: the Somme.

With the hurrying wind behind us, we reach the Somme before we expect to. There is the river below, running off toward the west: a quiet-looking stream, never very wide, meandering through fields and marshes. We cross it at Cléry and pass over Maricourt, where the British lines began. Ahead is the village of Mametz, and nearby Mametz Wood. How small the wood seems. I wonder if it was that size when Robert Graves fought there, found a dead Boche propped against a tree, and wrote a poem about him: "Big-bellied, spectacled, crop-haired, / Dribbling black blood from nose and beard."

From 2,000 feet on this bright clear day, we can see the entire battlefield—eighteen or twenty miles long, six or seven miles wide. Down there is the old Roman road running straight as a ruler the twelve miles from Albert to Bapaume. The British fought along it through the summer and autumn of 1916, and at the battle's end they were still short of their objective. So many lives lost, for such a little distance. But the whole battlefield seems too small to contain the 3 million men who fought there and suffered more than a million casualties—too small and too tidy. It is a flat piece of rural countryside, full of small villages and divided by roads and field boundaries, with the Somme on the south and the Ancre on the west, all lying very quietly this Sunday morning.

The war is nevertheless there—in the cemeteries and monuments, in the craters, in the visible marks of trenches that stretch out on both sides of the river. Our eyes are continually distracted by signs and yet more signs of the war. Anthony keeps exclaiming, "There's a cemetery there, there's another, there's a monument!" and wheeling and banking the plane, while I nervously think of the embarrassment of spinning in on a flight like this one, surviving the Second World War in the air, only to die in the First.

We cross the Lochnager Crater at La Boisselle, a hole as big as a meteorite might make—60,000 pounds of explosive blew up there on July 1, 1916—and approach the village of Thiepval. Nearby is the Memorial to the Missing, designed by the English architect Sir Edwin Lutyens (who also designed the monuments for the British war cemeteries: the Great War Stone and the Cross of Sacrifice). I am surprised at how ugly the memorial is—massive, brutal, and somehow irritatingly busy in its many planes and angles. I hadn't known that it was made of brick (all of the others that we've seen are of stone), and perhaps it's the brick that reminds me of an Edwardian railway station. I try to imagine what Lutyens thought that pile of bricks expressed, and decide that it is an instance of a good architect (probably a good man, too) defeated by the impossible problem of finding what *could* be said in the language of architecture about more than 70,000 dead men whose bodies are still missing, their bones scattered among those fields. There are tourists crossing the green lawn toward the monument as we pass, and I wonder how it strikes them, at ground level. Farther along, more tourists wave from the top of the Ulster Division tower. (The Ulsters advanced farther than any other division, about a mile; half of them were casualties, and they lost what ground they'd gained.) It's the first time that I've been aware of the war as a tourist attraction.

From Thiepval we cross the Ancre to Beaumont-Hamel, and the Newfoundland Memorial Park there. This must be the nearest thing existing to what a pilot would have seen during the war—not in 1916 while the battle was being fought, but afterward, in 1917 or 1918. The lines of the trenches remain here, not neatly sandbagged as at Vimy Ridge, but irregular, caving in on themselves, yet with their zigzag lines clearly visible. All around the trenches are the pits of shell holes, making the surface of the earth look like diseased flesh. There are no trees in this space, only a melancholy emptiness. It was on these bare slopes that on July 1, 1916, German machine guns cut down nearly the entire 1st Newfoundland Battalion.

The Somme, seen from the air, has been overwhelming—too many monuments, too many cemeteries. I'm at the controls now, and I bank round to the southwest, toward Amiens. Like so many soldiers on this front during the war, we will seek rest and a meal there, away from the battlefield. On the way we pass over Albert and see the golden figure of the Virgin atop the tower of the basilica. In 1915 a German shell hit the figure, leaving it hanging at a precarious angle over the town, and a legend sprang up that when it fell the war would end. In August of 1918 the Germans took the town. British artillery shelled the church tower, and the Virgin fell, but the war continued. After the war the basilica and the golden Virgin were restored. "She still looks a bit bent to me," Anthony says, as we fly past. Farther along, just north of Corbie, where the Somme and the Ancre meet, we pass the spot where the Red Baron, Manfred von Richthofen, was shot down. He was the heroic enemy of my boyhood, when I read *G-8 and His Battle Aces* and dreamed of Spads and Fokkers. I give him a dip of the wings.

1:40 P.M.: north of Amiens.

After lunch at the Amiens Airport, we are off again under a lowering sky. A solid overcast slopes down to a black horizon at the Channel, and there are scattered patches of clouds, like bunches of dirty wool, drifting below us. It's as though the fair weather had held as long as we needed it, but now that we are done with our searching after the war, the weather has turned. My spirits sink.

There are other places along our route that will remind us of other wars: Crécy is over there toward the coast, and we will pass over Agincourt on our way back to Calais; north of Calais is Dunkirk. A lot of wars have been fought on this corner of France, though no sign of any of them is visible now. And I wonder if perhaps that isn't best, to let the earth erase the marks that battles make on it and revert to what it has always been. We have seen so many monuments in these two days, so many rows of identical gravestones, so many crosses; and they have seemed, from the air, just patches of dead whiteness, defacing the natural life colors of the earth. And in the end, what testimony do they offer about war? That it kills in terrible numbers. And that human beings desire to preserve something of their dead: a body in a grave, if there is a body; if there is not, then a name on a stone. But something.

As for the other marks of war, they are obliterated in time by nature and by the persistence of ordinary human needs—the need to build, to make things grow, to get on with life. Unless artificially preserved, the Great War's ruination of fields and towns has nearly disappeared. To the circling eye above, there are only some slowly closing holes in the earth and the fading chalk trench lines.

3:35 P.M.: Calais.

We must land again at Calais to clear customs. The customs man is by now an old friend. We have been to Verdun? He lifts his shoulders in a Gallic shrug. "Ah," he says, "la guerre. La guerre." As we leave the field on the last leg of our journey, the sky is beginning to clear; far ahead of us, on the English side of the Channel, the clouds open, pouring down golden afternoon light on the cliffs and the sea, though on the French side the earth is still shadowed. We pass one last military cemetery south of the town, and then the vast workings of the Channel Tunnel entrance, a geometric swirl of lines and raw earth that looks like a huge engineer's drawing made of sand—a worse disfiguring of the landscape than any mark of war we have seen.

By the time we reach Dungeness and take our final heading along the coast toward home we are in bright sunlight, and England looks the way William Blake saw it, a green and pleasant land. There is one more battlefield down there, to remind us of the intention of our flight. We pass over the town of Battle, which is on the site of the Battle of Hastings. Today is the anniversary of that battle, and below us, in the grounds of Battle Abbey, Englishmen in medieval costume are reenacting it. It's a nice day for playing at war, but we don't pause. I wonder, as I fly on, whether any of those dressed-up men has seen the graves at Tyne Cot.

4:45 P.M.: Shoreham Airport.

I let down through scattered cumulus clouds over the field. The air is full of other small planes, returning from their own weekend adventures, and the flight controller is sharp and abrupt as he directs them in the pattern. I join the circle, fifth in line behind a Cessna; swing out over the sea, which is blue and glinting in the sun, and back across the beach; and turn in toward the strip. I land and taxi across the grass to the hangar. I'm tired, and my feelings, here at the flight's end, are tangled and contradictory. The flying has been the intense and special pleasure that it has been in my life for nearly fifty years, and I'm sorry it's over; but I'm also pleased to be home, and the ground has reassuring solidity. I have spent two days looking down at the story of war that is written on the French earth, and I feel heavy with the sadness of cemeteries. But I think I know something now about what it was like on the Western Front. The war for me has a landscape.

I cut the engine, and step down onto the English earth.

*

First *published in* MHQ: The Quarterly Journal
of Military History *(Summer 1992).*

Index of Names and Titles